editor assistant: Stephan May

cover: Léonard de Vinci, *Vulve*, 1504/09

special thanks to

Marianne Alphant, Alban Barre, Christine Buci-Glucksman, Françoise Gange, Catherine Malabou, Vanessa Mitrani, Elsa Olu, Anne de Villepoix.

and also

Louise Bourgeois, Judy Chicago, Tracey Emin, Valie Export, Elke Krystufek, Shigeko Kubota, Zoe Leonard, Léa Lublin, Sarah Lucas, Annette Messager, Jenny Saville, Carolee Scheemann, Kiki Smith, Yves Trémorin, Faith Wilding, Sue Williams, and Ronald Feldman Fine Arts, Brooklyn Museum of Art, White Cube.

ouvrage aidé par le Ministère français chargé de la Culture

3, rue Beautreillis
75004 Paris
France

website : http://www.disvoir.com
e-mail : disvoir@aol.com

ISBN 2-914563-10-8

PRINTED IN EUROPE

KEEP THIS SEX OUT OF MY SIGHT

this series edited by

DANIÈLE RIVIÈRE

in the same series

CONTEMPORARY PRACTICES: ART AS EXPERIENCE

Paul Ardenne, Pascal Beausse, Laurent Goumarre

TECHNO: AN ARTISTIC AND POLITICAL LABORATORY OF THE PRESENT

Michel Gaillot, Jean-Luc Nancy, Michel Maffesoli

SOUND AND THE VISUAL ARTS

Jean-Yves Bosseur

IN FAVOUR OF TODAY'S ART

François Dagognet

CLEMENT GREENBERG BETWEEN THE LINES

Thierry de Duve

KEEP THIS SEX OUT OF MY SIGHT

ELVAN ZABUNYAN

CHRYSTEL BESSE

ARLETTE FONTAN

FRANÇOISE GAILLARD

MARIE-JOSEPH BERTINI

CONTENTS

**Translated from the French*

Anatomy / Autonomy

Art theory in the 20th Century has talked at length, often in a rhetoric form, on the place occupied by the female figure and the numerous visual representations stemming from it. However, until the propositions and revendications of the feminists during the Seventies in Europe and the United States, little analyses have succeeded in setting down in a critical fashion an art history which would no longer be exclusively male (integrating only a few rare female references when they were impossible to avoid) but thought as an inclusive entity in which the question of genders would be assimilated into the creation without being considered as peripheral. One notices, nevertheless, that, despite the greater involvement of female artists and/or intellectuals in the art territory, the problematics remains with us in a cultural field where Western patriarchal ideas are only partially questioned. To choose to speak about female artists when one is an art theoretician is thus a form of subjective involvement in which the different modalities of visual reading will have to be reflected by clearly including the historical, cultural and social parameters while being attentive to not just constructing a parallel history. To go beyond an established rigidity—notably the one to assimilate a research on the female artist and her sexual parts to a form of sectarianism—there is no need for justifications, the elements of response are and remain affirmative.

Subjectivity and construction

Within the continuity of figurative painting and sculpture, throughout the history of visual representation, the female body has become an experimental surface where the integrity of the subject has been largely hidden. The images of multiple, but also multiplied, women, mainly caught in the male gaze, have constructed a contemporary and daily visual landscape through their omnipresence in the world of art, photography and cinema, but also, in a more commercial way, within the media, advertising and fashion. *Objectified*, the woman represented, even sublimated, has begun to lose her identity to transform herself into mediation for a society based on show. Through the representation of her body, the woman as "object" has only been able to find her identity again through a process of visualization. It is that moment of creation when the gaze one casts on oneself specifically de-constructs the stereotype of the woman-object and underlines her position as a subject through the assertion of subjectivity. Numerous reflections carefully considered in the Seventies (the period that marks in an exemplary fashion that passage to subjectivity) links the phenomenon to a positive recognition of one's own sexual parts as a determining and central aspect of the biological body. "Woman touches herself in and of herself without any need for mediation, and before there is any way to distinguish activity from passivity. Woman 'touches herself' all the time, without anyone being able to forbid her to do so, for her genitals are formed of two lips in continuous embrace. Thus, within herself, she is already two—but not divisible into one(s)—that caress each other," declares Luce Irigaray in *Ce sexe qui n'en est pas un.*[1] This very physical description by the psychoanalyst is also a way to counteract the irreversible effects of Freudian analyses which have ultimately succeeded in making their mark on the Western collective unconscious with the idea of a "weaker sex". As the woman's genitalia are defined for Sigmund Freud as "absence" (of

[1] Luce Irigaray, *Ce sexe qui n'en est pas un*, Paris: Editions de Minuit, 1977, p.24. Translated in *This Sex Which Is Not One*, New York: Cornell University Press, 1985.

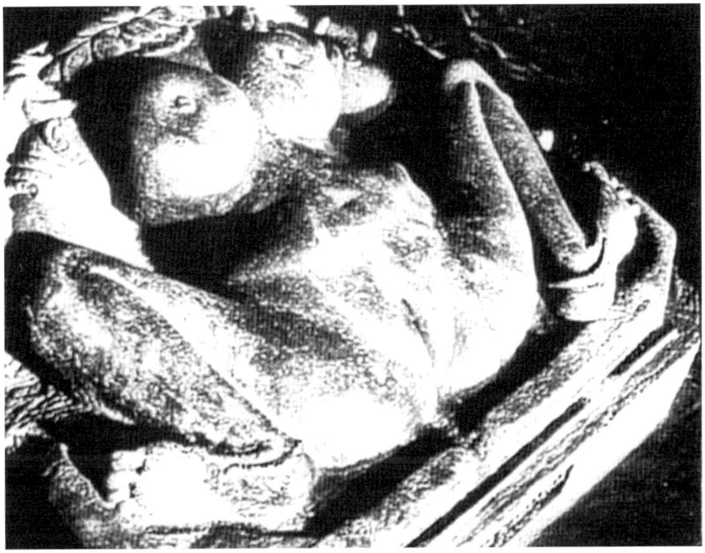

1

3

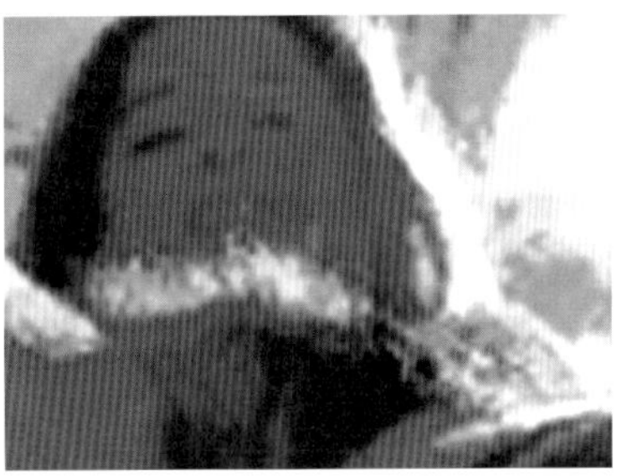

2

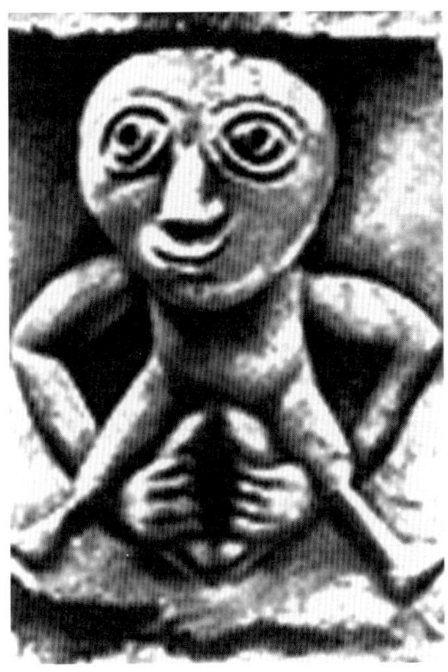

A little flashback for our contemporaries. There was a time when sex was free and the act of union between male and female was considered sacred. The female sexual organs were the door to the divine.

the phallus) or "cavity", they become, following that logic, empty elements "to be filled". The interest a woman can bring to bear on her body is often interpreted as a form of narcissism while in the defined frame of pictorial or photographic parameters, the representation of her own sexual parts is a very simple way to re-appropriate her intimacy by extracting it from the male hegemony.

From The origin of the world *to the origin of the self*

When Khalil Bey, the Turkish Ambassador in Saint Petersburg, a collector of art and erotic objects, commissioned *The origin of the world* from Gustave Courbet in 1866, the image of that female sexual part painted close-up and almost at human size was primarily destined for the desiring gaze of a man. Noting the history of art through its multiple enigmas and analyses, *The origin of the world* has always been interpreted in two ways: for its eroticism and its maternity. However, that interpretation does not really apply to the reality of the representation if one leaves aside those two approaches. Framed in a way as to underline the slight roundness of the pubis covered in hair, the construction of the painting is conceived following "anti-narrative strategies", to quote Linda Nochlin in her explanation of Manet's work. The representation remains faithful to reality in terms of the painter's speciality and strangely seems to resist stereotyping. That quasi-photographic framing accentuates the true to life nature of the pose, which is not in keeping with an erotic lasciviousness. Further, that sexual part is no longer regarded as being the source of maternity. It is simply there, between the thighs. It exists in its relationship to the body. It is still responsible for its status as subject. The work of analysis has still to be done. To underline the subjectivity of that female sexual part, even if it has more in common with male experiences, rocks the theoretical approach towards a new interpretation: the reflexivity of the female gaze.

Deciphering the notion of representation, Kate Linker, in her famous essay, "Representation and Sexuality", written in 1983, insists on the importance of the production of meaning: "the subject is at once placed in, or by, the discourse and constructed in, or by, the discourse. (...) This constitution of identity such that man is viewer, woman viewed, and the viewing process a mode of domination and control has been applied to the tradition of the female nude such that it can be integrated into the history of art".[2] Going back to a remark made by Jacques Lacan in 1958, Linker quotes: "images and symbols *for* the woman cannot be isolated from images and symbols *of* the woman... It is representation, the representation of feminine sexuality (...) which conditions how it comes into play"[3]. In this reflexive process, the inversion is made through a history of gazes which shift. Lacan's position joins the viewpoint of the sexual parts represented by Courbet, there is no longer any separation between what belongs to the woman and what represents her but, at the same time, what disposseses her of her essence. For the woman cannot have a view of her own sexual parts like this one, and, if one goes back, at the same time as contradicting it, to the famous Lacanian phrase, "I cannot see myself seeing myself", the woman is compelled to see herself look at her intimate parts for she cannot have an "entire" vision of them simply by bending forward. That way, she only sees her pubis and her labia majora, the rest only being visible with the help of a reflecting object, after having parted her legs. The distancing necessitates the space of the mirror which reflects the image. The mirror itself becomes the image because it has created it. The model is extracted from an obsolete functionality in order to construct a new way to gaze on herself. The game of gazes imposed by the mirror is apparent intrinsincally to the form that can take, for the woman, an auto-representation of her sexual parts, but also of her desire.

[2] Kate Linker, "Representation and Sexuality", first appeared in Parachute No 32, autumn 1983, pp. 12-23. Also in *Art after Modernism, rethinking Representation*, New York: The New Museum of Contemporary Art, 1984, p. 392

[3] *ibid.*, p. 39.

4

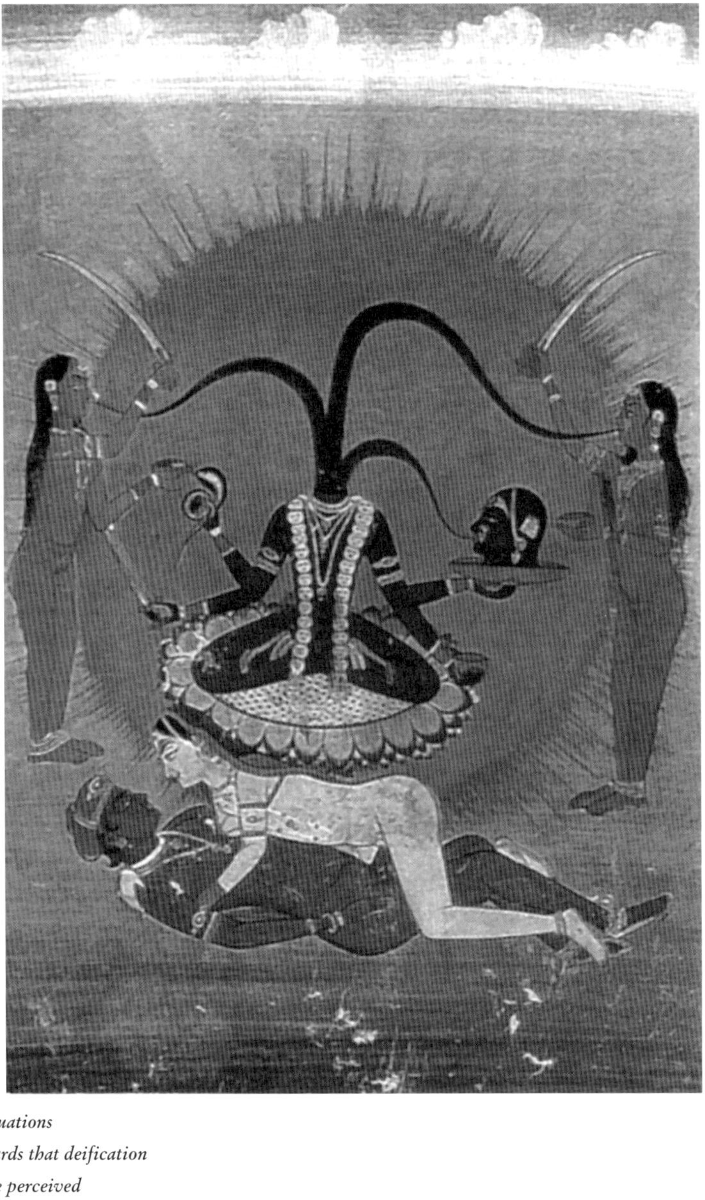

Even menstruations
worked towards that deification
for they were perceived
as extraordinary energies.

From gaze to touch

Irigaray has a frontal analysis of the difference between female and male desire. According to her, "woman's desire would not be expected to speak the same language as man's; woman's desire has doubtless been submerged by the logic that has dominated the West since the time of the Greeks. Within this logic, the predominance of the gaze, and of the discrimination and indivualization of form, is particularly foreign to female eroticism. Woman takes pleasure more from touching than from looking, and her entry into a dominant scopic economy signifies, again, her consignment to passivity: she will be the beautiful object to be looked at"[4] However, that "beautiful object to be looked at" is also the one which does not have the right to live its jouissance. Few indeed if any erotic representation of the woman speaks about her jouissance. The cliché of the submissive woman, victim and sexual object, is the one that dominates. Her subordination to male desire is the only one that exists visually. In the patriarchal order, male power passes through the regressive mode of repression, even of the most immediate, violence. As far as rape, the ultimate form of its supremacy. Referring to the famous painting by Delacroix, *Death of Sardanapalus* (1827), Linda Nochlin writes, analysing the creative process of the painter: "it is obvious that by painting such a subject with as much sensual appetite, erotic panache and truthfulness, Delacroix was on the verge of describing in an unvarnished way one of the most explosive fantasies, and thus one of the most carefully repressed, of the patriarchal discourse on desire: the revendication for oneself of the murder and sexual possession as absolute jouissance."[5] "Until proven to the contrary, the 19th century has simply not known art, and even less 'great art', devoted to the needs, wishes or erotic fantasies of women. That the erotic object is breasts or buttocks, shoes or corset, a question of pose or archetype, those images of delectation or sexual provocation have always been created on the subject

[4] Luce Irigaray, *op.cit.*, p.25

[5] Linda Nochlin, "Femmes, Art et Pouvoir", in *Femmes, Art et Pouvoir* (1989), Nîmes: Editions Jacqueline Chambon, 1993, p.24

of women, for the pleasure of men and by men," Nochlin also notes, before adding: "the images of the male translate power, possession, domination, and those of the female, submission, passivity, availability. The language of love itself confirms it as much as the erotic imagery of the visual arts."[6]

The experience of the body, the experience of sexual organs, a visual history

To fill that gap and contradict that position, much later, in the mid-Sixties, female artists began to work on their bodies and their sexual organs with a view to asserting their sexual identity as much as their artistic one. For a long while, the confusion has been to think the second was used as a pretext for the first, when for most of the time those two identities determine themselves in a parallel and complementary way in the creative process. To consider the supremacy of gender on the artistic work produced by systematically returning the analyses to the most hackneyed clichés is worn out. By way of prelude to the catalogue of the exhibition *Sexual Politics* in 1996, we can read this quotation from the feminist artist Faith Wilding: "There's lots of vaginas in our work, but it is not about vagina. Rather, we are inventing a new form of language radiating a female power which cannot be conveyed in any other way at this time. (...) As women artists we are presenting an image of woman's body and spirit as that which cannot and must not be colonized either sexually, economically or politically."[7]

When the woman who decides to commit herself in a performance work talks about her own body as a material, she reinvents new modalities of representation and reading, at a time when the forms of visual expression are already mutating. In 1965, during the "Perpetual

[6] Linda Nochlin, "Erotisme et images du féminin au XIXe", in *op cit.*, pp.192-197

[7] Faith Wilding, prelude to *Sexual Politics: Judy Chicago's "Dinner Party"* in *Feminist Art History, Berkeley*, Los Angeles: University of California Press, 1996.

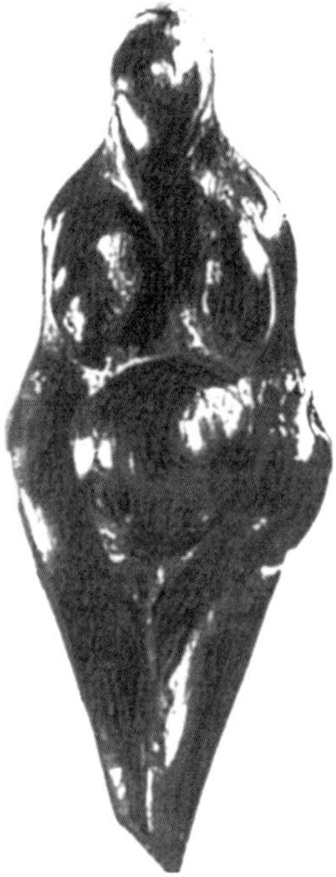

5

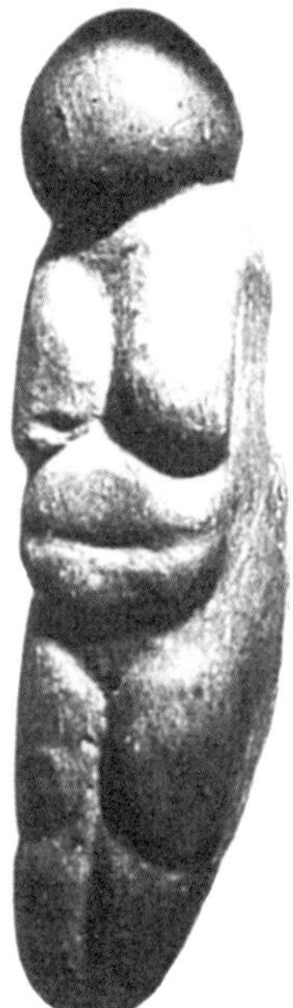

8

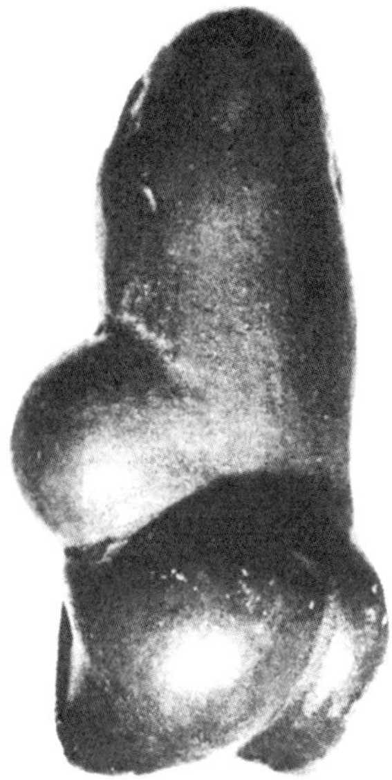

7

But that female hegemony
was gradually overtaken
through the emergence
of the patriarchal power,
represented by
the phallic aspect of some statuettes...

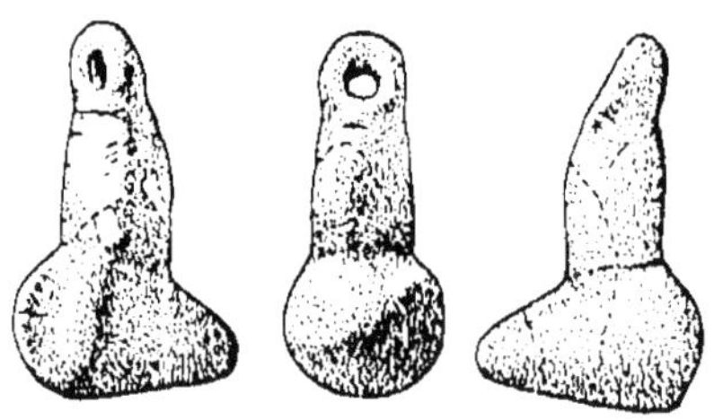

9

...even becoming phallocentric.

Fluxfest", a Fluxus festival held in New York, the Japanese artist, Shigeko Kubota (born in 1937) created a performance that she called *Vaginal Painting*. Voluntarily defined as an "action painting", making explicit reference to the "drippings" method of Jackson Pollock, the artist's performance consisted in spreading a large sheet of paper on the ground and painting red stripes with a paintbrush attached to her underwear. The photograph of this performance shows her squatting, her short dress pulled up her thighs, the paintbrush looking as if coming from her vagina. That way she created a deliberately female method of gestural painting. For Shigeko Kubota, whose artistic research is inscribed in a reflection on the mainly male Western art, and whose process is very different from Japanese art, *Vaginal Painting* was also a parody of Yves Klein's anthropometrics created at the end of the Fifties, in which the female body was transformed into a human paintbrush. To question the art of Yves Klein, as has been done numerous times by American feminist theories on the art of performance created by women, under that more misogynous angle, was not readily imaginable in France. The love of women as muses is more often underlined than their bodies as pictorial function reduced to breasts, belly and thighs. In Europe, as a matter of fact, criticism remains somewhat hostile to that practise of "Body Art", considering it as regressive and infantalizing.[8] The criterion of identity (that this one is sexual, ethnic or racial) as a form of analysis constituent of a visual practise has yet to be integrated into the majority of European countries. What results is a total absence of any form of questioning of the artistic authority of some painters. Yves Klein is one of them. Only Anglo-Saxon analyses have questioned more closely the use that Klein made of the female body. By using her sexual organs as a source of inspiration, Shigeko Kubota researched the cultural definitions of the female genitals in Western culture while provoking in a very direct way an upheaval of artistic acceptance.

[8] See on this subject passages in Lucy R. Lippard, "*The Pains and Pleasures of Rebirth: European and American Women's Body Art*", in The Pink Glass Swan, *Selected feminist essays on art*, New York: The New Press, 1995, pp.99-113.

The orgasm as form

In the same way, when Barbara Hammer (born in 1939) shot her film *Multiple Orgasms* in 1976, she asked about the contemporary modalities of the female sexual organs and female sexuality. The image that fills the frame is a superimposition of several shots, the interior of a cave on the image of the artist masturbating. The genitals close up, lips open, is caressed by fingers. The artist appropriates the words of Luce Irigaray when she talks about the female genitals being two lips in continuous embrace. She underlines her desire to express herself in the form of multiple superimposed images and films shown in loops.

Parallel to the social demands of her daily life, sexual pleasure becomes, for the woman, one of the most important forms of her freedom. The artist expresses that by shifting it towards the visual sphere. Contrary to pornographic representations where absent desire and non-existent pleasure become the parameters of the jouissance spectacle, it is in a simple and frontal fashion that artists reveal these sensations, visually invisible (the pleasure is internal), *by giving themselves to be looked at*. As if to show oneself giving oneself pleasure could become a way to assert a sexual accomplishment that is first of all solitary. The presence of the man is indeed obliterated in most representations, as if the stages had to be reached gradually. When the female artist caressses herself, even if she does it in order to register the image of her action, she does not simulate. The title of the artistic proposition sets the tone. The multiple orgasms of Barbara Hammer, a committed feminist and producer of experimental films involving gay culture, are such because of the editing technique and her superimposition of images; but the mental image born with the idea of *Multiple Orgasms* is also the revendication for an entire jouissance.

In 1967, the Austrian artist, Valie Export (born in 1940), shot an 8mm film lasting 30 seconds that she called *Orgasm*. The relationship to temporarility is like a collision. One counts the seconds, the duration of the pleasure. One seizes pleasure in its supreme state. Valie Export, living at that time in Germany, is one of the first female artists to have thrown herself into guerrilla-style actions which stamped the history of contemporary art because of their extreme nature. In 1969, dressed in a black shirt, a pair of trousers whose crutch had been cut away to reveal her naked genitals, hair dishevelled, a machine-gun in hand, she entered a porno cinema in Munich and performed her piece *Genital Panic*.[9] By associating the visual relationship to the sexual relationship as established with regard to a pornographic film, she decided to upset the spectators in their function as passive voyeurs by inviting them to "touch" her genitals while threatening them with the gun. None gave in to her request, choosing instead to leave the cinema silently. The violence of the performance lay above all in its idea. In an implacable way Valie Export questioned the parameters of genital visibility as imagined in pornographic representations, but also in its reality. If many women, by choosing to use their body as their material, have shown themselves naked in public performances, here the artist laid bare one of the most intimate parts of her body without revealing the rest. That way she destroyed all assimilation with the traditional female nude model which could be recaptured in some situations. She asserted herself as a fully aware rebel and integrated her action into a particularly loaded international political context. Beyond the representation, the risk she took in *Genital Panic* was real.

Sexual organs as artistic material

By starting to intervene in a social and political field until then reserved for men, female artists articulated the consequences of domination. They provoked situations where their bodies expressed their subjectivity. Hannah Wilke (1940-1993), originally a sculptor, began to create a work in which she associated different visual materials with a body and vaginal iconography. Between 1978 and 1984, Hannah Wilke

[9] For a fairly complete analysis of the work of Valie Export, see Roswitha Mueller, *Valie Export, Fragments of the Imagination*, Bloomington, Indianapolis: Indiana University Press, 1994.

11

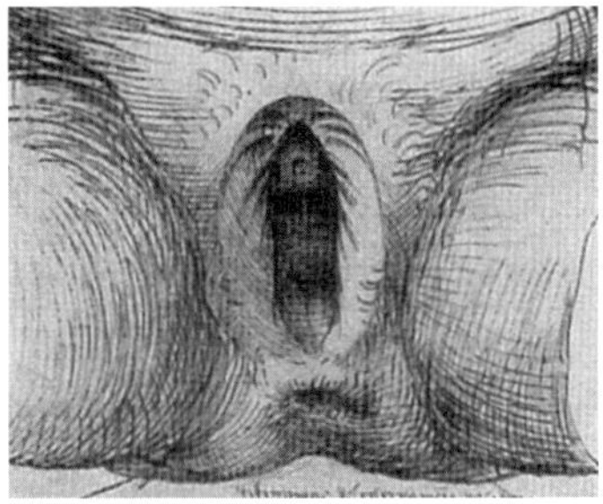

10

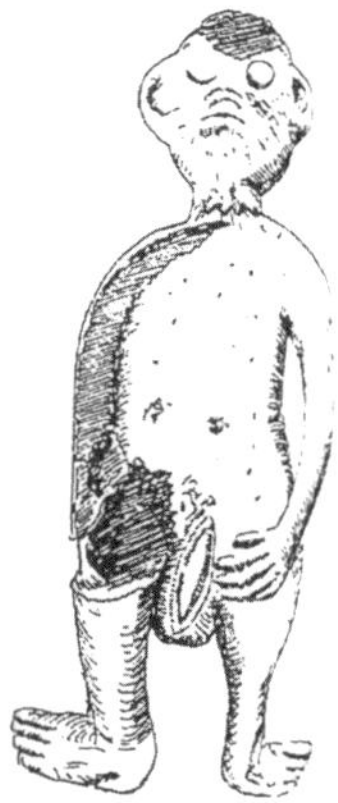

14

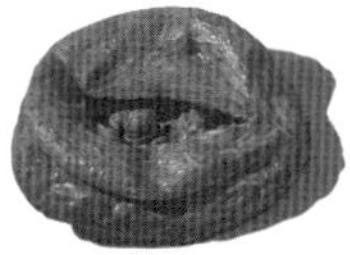

12

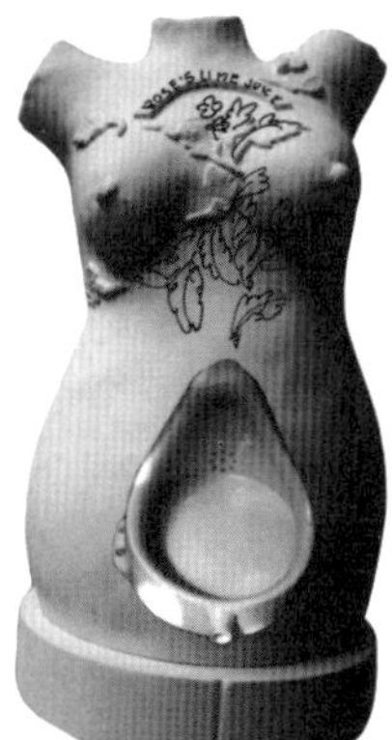

13

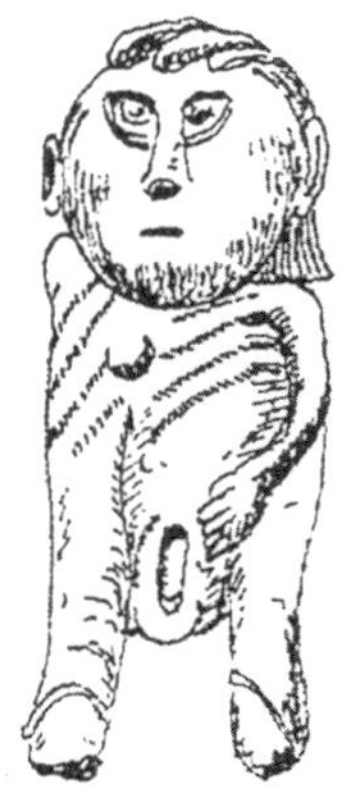

The patriarchal power,
reinforced by monotheistic religions,
looked at the female sexual organs with a look
that never ceased debasing and necrotizing it.

created performances recorded by photography and video in which she placed herself in different situations, all linked to a famous quotation by a male artist. One of the first was entitled *What Does This Represent? What do you Represent?* The first question took a quote by the painter Ad Reinhardt dating from 1945. The artist presented herself seated on the floor in a corner, naked, legs spread wide, wearing high-heeled shoes, and with "boys" toys (mostly miniature weapon-like toys). Her genitals were at the centre of the image, thus of the composition. Between inscribing in the history of art and doubt on the question of the model, that series Wilke called *So Help Me Hannah* interpreted an assumed reflexivity of the self-portrait long tested by the artist.

Photography and video become the essential relay of performance, whether public or private, and it is often thanks to those document-images that the artistic productions circulate. Carolee Schneemann's action, *Interior Scroll*, has been reproduced numerous times, allowing her to be recognized at the heart of the history of art that integrates women. In 1975, in New York, a year after writing her essay "Istory of a Girl Pornographer", in which she describes in critical form her female status *seen* more as an *image* than as *a woman making images*, the artist created in front of an exclusively female audience one of her most complete performances.[10] Having succeeded in harmonising her sexual organs and her work, Carolee Schneemann asserted her position as female artist, underlining the importance of a personal sexual freedom. For *Interior Scroll*, she appeared wrapped in a sheet that she let drop to reveal her naked body. She put traces of paint on her face and different parts of her body, then indicated that she was going to read passages from her book *Cezanne, she was a great painter*. After, she climbed on a table, let the book drop and began to extract a long scroll from her vagina. That scroll became the narrative function of both an interiority and a relationship to history and creation. The text written on the strip of paper extracted

[10] Carolee Schneemann created her performance *Interior Scroll* twice, the first time on the 29th August 1975 in New York in the framework of a manifestation entitled "Women Here and Now", the second on the 4th September 1977, in Colarado in the framework of the "Telluride Film Festival".

from her body was a quotation of feminist texts that composed her visual work *Kitsch's Last Meal* (1973-1976). In an explicit way, Carolee Schneemann appropriated the archetype of the snake as sexual symbol, permitting the cliché conferred upon it to be turned upside down. Starting from an analysis of the "istory" of art (the artist never uses the term "history" because she refuses the "male" gender (his) in the word) and the symbolism of the snake, she has reflected on a "vulvic space" since 1960. "I thought of the vagina in many ways —physically, conceptually, as a sculptural form, an architectural referent, the source of the sacred knowledge, ecstasy, birth passage, transformation".[11] The snake as external model and symbol of passage makes the invisible (the internal part of the vagina which cannot be seen) visible (the scroll which unrolls). From Cézanne, as one of the fathers of modern painting, to Carolee Schneemann's performance, through references to the female symbolism of the Goddess since Antiquity as thought by the artist, the elements of analysis are juxtaposed. In this work her vagina becomes the vessel of a knowledge. Without any form of derision, she re-centres the idea of the sexual organs as being at the heart of corporality. That position in which the genitals become the material both for thought and pleasure is recurrent in a certain number of female artists who will make a positive form of the term that defines the female sexual organs in a pejorative way: *cunt* in English, *con* in French. In 1973, the American critic, Cindy Nemser even invented the term "cunt art" to define feminist art which used an iconography "of the vulva". At the same time, critics were divided concerning the possibility of inscribing the image of the female sexual organs as image and exclusive symbol of woman, in particular because that iconography developed a form of essentialist analysis. It was the monumental work of Judy Chicago (born in 1939), created between 1974 and 1979, entitled *The Dinner Party*, that especially provoked many questions and polemics. As a tribute to the woman in History, Chicago set a triangular table on which thirty nine plates were

[11] Carolee Schneemann, "Interior Scroll" (1977), in Carolee Schneemann, *Imaging her Erotics, Essays, Interviews, Projects*, Cambridge, MA; London: The MIT Press, 2002, pp.153-161

16

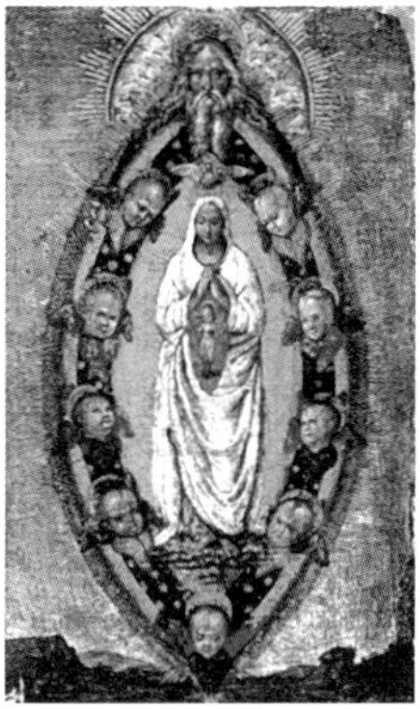

17

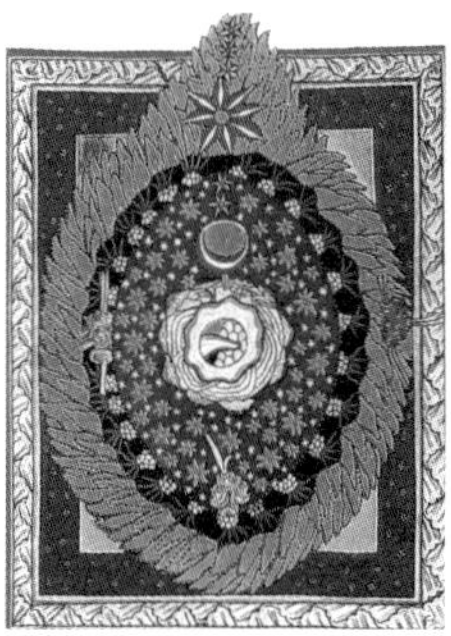

15

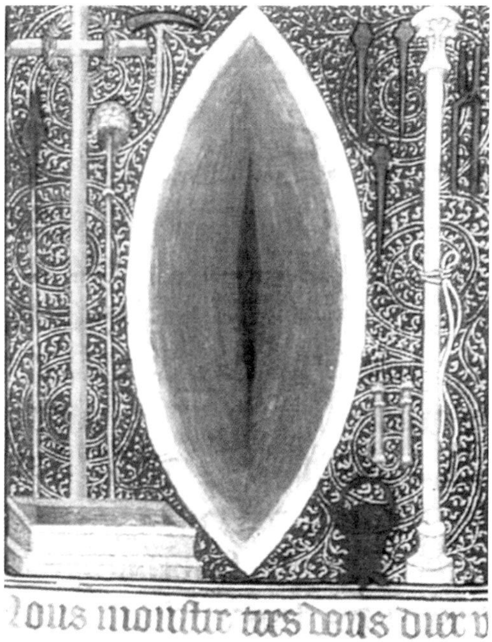

There were only a few representations of esoteric nature that would attempt to rehabilitate the idolatry of the female sexual organs by using some iconographic subtleties....

18

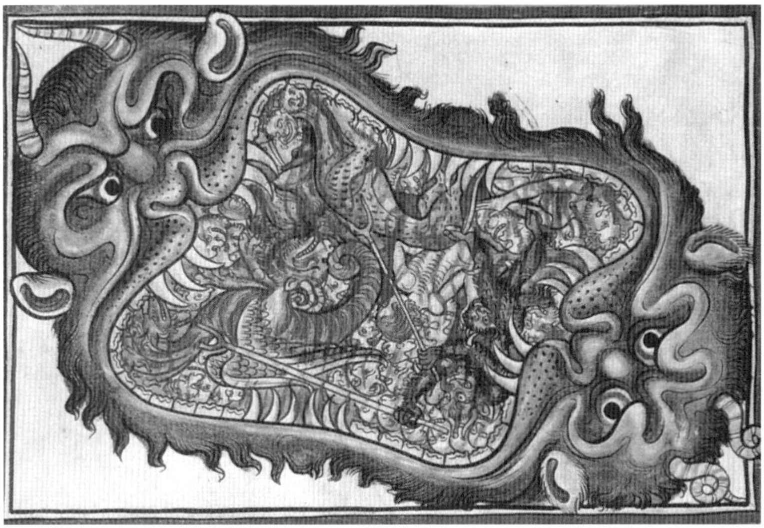

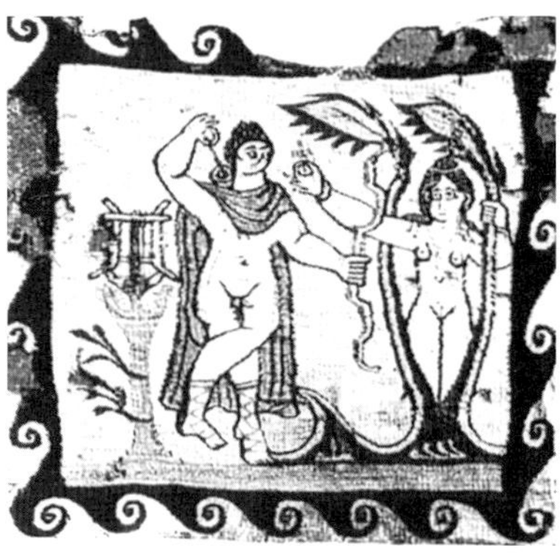

19

Incriminated by
the primitive church,
the female sexual organs,
instead of being made sacred,
became indissociable from the
ill-fated and
mortal day of
the original sin: the Fall of the
spirit into substance.

set at regular intervals, each of these plates being the figuration of a petal-vulva. The imagery was very close to the flowers painted by Georgia O'Keeffe. Each plate was the effigy of a famous woman, whether writer, artist or historical figure. Judy Chicago's work posed the successive stages of the origins of a society at first matriarchal which, constrained, gave way to a patriarchal organization with, finally, its consequences on women's oppression. However, these representations loaded with symbolic ornaments have been seen as an obsolete form of women's representation at a time when the slogan "the personnal is political" brought as much importance to individual commitment as to the collective one. The personages of Gertrude Stein or Virginia Woolf, as emblematic of feminism, were transformed into gaping and coloured sexual organs made in bas-refief. The questions raised at the end of this work also concerned one of the plates representing the famous black American slave, Sojourner Truth, who did not appear in the shape of a vulva, but three faces.[12]

That confrontation of the image of the woman with that of her sexual organs in the work of Judy Chicago, despite its importance in art history, does not mark a form of preponderent theoretical analysis. That work does not question concretely the problematics linked to questions of social or economical order, it remains in the field of representation. Once the stage of surprise is over, the plates-sexual organs are not even obscene, they are reduced to being passive figures. The use of the female sexual organs, of the *cunt*, is nevertheless visible in the art practise until recent times, more often in a figurative form.

[12] It is Alice Walker, especially, author of *The Colour Purple* who expressed heavy criticism on that precise point. According to her, the artist's difficulty in representing the sexual organs of a black woman is revelatory to the position occupied by Afro-american women in American history. Black women would not have a sexual organ. In a significant way, the explanation can lead to several contradictory interpretations insofar as the feminism of white women and the feminism of black women was made up in a very different historical and political perspective. White women, for example, started by claiming the right to work while black women, as soon as they had arrived on American soil, have never stopped working. See Alice Walker, "One Child of One's Own: A Meaningful Digression within the Work(s)", in *Search of Our Mother's Garden: Womanist Prose*, 1983

About the love of a multiple self: the personal is political

More conceptual propositions have emerged in a subtle way, for example, the work of Zoe Leonard (born in 1961), presented at the Documenta IX in Kassel in 1992. Exhibiting in the seven rooms of the Neue Gallery's collection of paintings from the 18th Century, her first intervention was to withdraw all the male portraits and landscape paintings and to leave only the portraits of women in their golden frames. In the empty spaces, she placed nineteen black and white photographs of the female sexual organ with a hand caressing it. The contrast created immediately told a story, that of the woman, of course, but also of her representation—the face/portrait, the sexual organ/portrait—from painting to photography. Beyond the surprise that this comparing between centuries and forms can provoke, it is a very radical presence that emerges. Here too the woman is the one who gives herself pleasure (in this case the artist when she creates her work) and pleasures herself (by touching), the anonymous and universal sexual organ becomes the one of all women. Without any form of exhibitionism usually associated with the representation of genitals is expressed on the contrary a form of modesty which gives itself to be seen. The paradox is to reach that integrity while revealing oneself through the most intimate part of one's body. For it is not sufficient to show the sexual organ, to see the sexual organ alone does not mean a thing. On the other hand, inscribed in a context where the form has a critical or poetic function, the meaning reveals itself more explicitly, it is more free. The untitled "hanging" of Zoe Leonard was close to that. The time-space which separates the 1970s from the 1990s integrates the artistic propositions of women with many more difficulties of analysis. A sexual organ photographed or painted in a period of social and political revendications does not carry the same visual meaning as the sexual organ as shown today at the dawn of the third millenium. At a time when the references of the body are more than ever lost in an accepted form of vulgarity, the indirect consequences of sexual liberation have almost locked the image of the woman into the

20

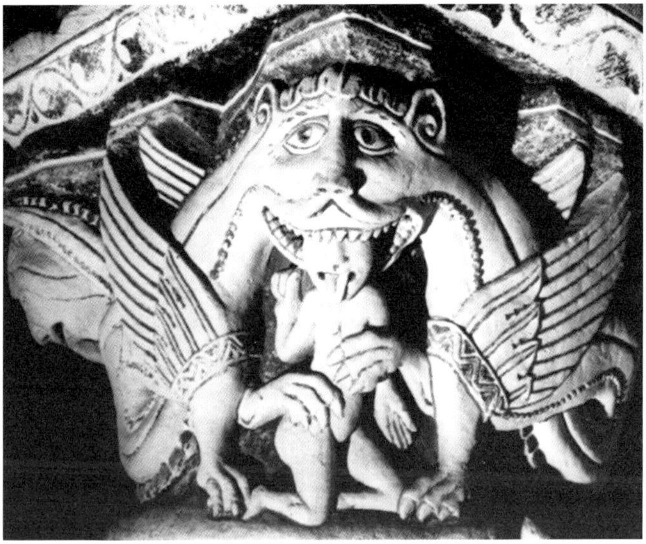

21

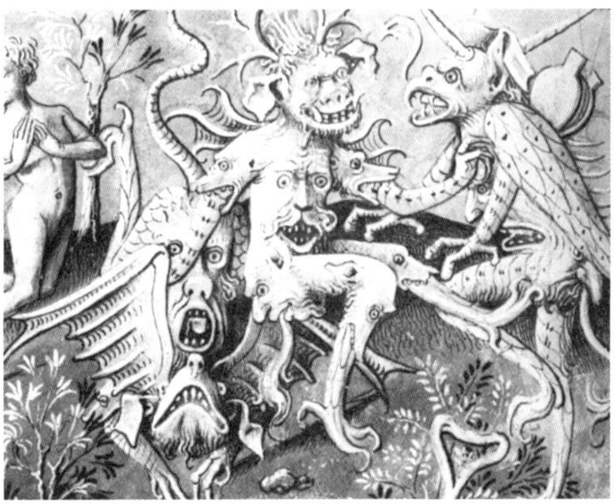

22

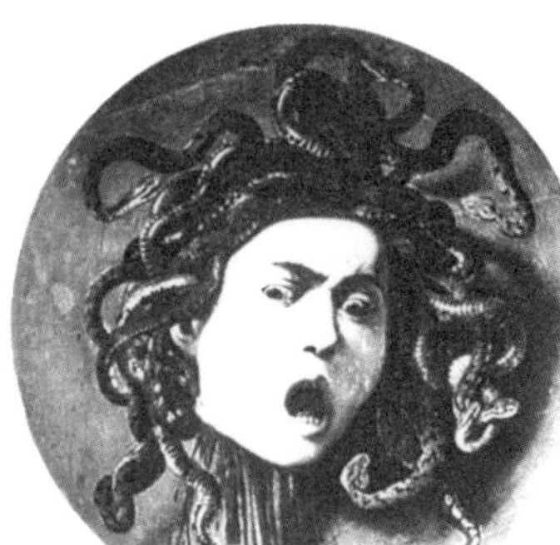

Women were thus dangerous by "nature"
and provided with a big vaginal mouth
armed with sharp teeth...

most regressive ensemble. If freedom is sought by women in an accomplishment of their sexuality detached from the metaphor of lack, emptiness and suffering, the unbearable, even unendurable proliferation of stereotyped and sexualized images of the female body responding to male canons are causing a brutal backlash. Pornography today has become for some women a way to assert a non-subordinate position while that form of representation of principally heterosexual sexuality only re-enforces the subordinate role of the woman, her desire or her jouissance. How to conceive a satisfying relation to one's body when the actions add up to a mechanical copulation, ejaculation on the face and, often as not, total submission? To use pornography as a possibility to liberate the sexual organ and its practise is a way to deny the legacy of a long and tricky revendication which asserts itself throughout independance and autonomy. The difficulty to think about the question comes too from the fact that the elements of the discourse quickly break free from the rhetoric to contradict each other. The increase in pornographic images beyond their reserved area penetrates the heart of an accessible popular culture (via the media, the distribution of films on video and Internet) in order to (supposedly) liberate sexual relationships. More visible, they are even more partitioned in a distressing unilateral imagery. The insistence of some women when they appropriate a form of pornographic sexuality (understood as under the mainly quasi-male masturbatory gaze) and think of it as somehow salvatory, only locks up their own pleasure. They see themselves seeing the sexual act. They give more importance to the seeing than the doing. They see the sexual organs, they don't make love. The personal stories of women and their sexual organs can be offered to view, can be transmitted by narratives, can be listened to, can be imagined.

But their interpretation carries more than one meaning: the seeing of a vulva, ready and waiting for a penis in a film is pornographic; a woman who opens herself to view and, firstly, her own, in a desire to counteract the other discriminatory viewing, is a space of resistance. The "object" represented is the same, the inherent subject, different. In one there is disrespect for one's own person, in the other there is a consciousness of her emancipation. The female sexual organ is not a form. "But, *woman has sex organs more or less everywhere*. She finds pleasure (jouit) almost anywhere. (...) The geography of her pleasure is far more diversified, more multiple in its differences, more complex, more subtle, than is imagined..."[13]

[13] Luce Irigaray, *op. cit*., p. 30.

24

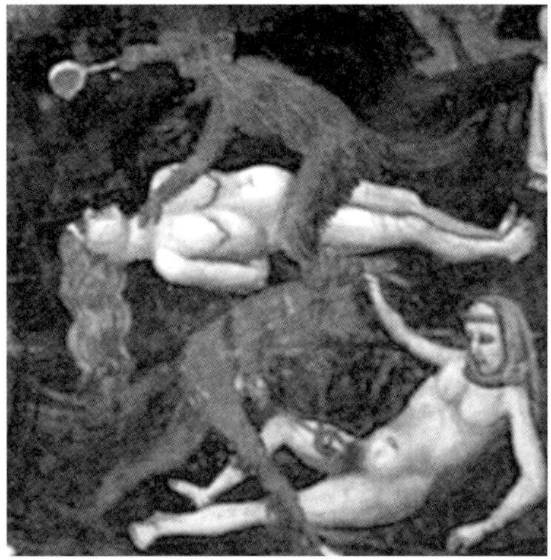

23

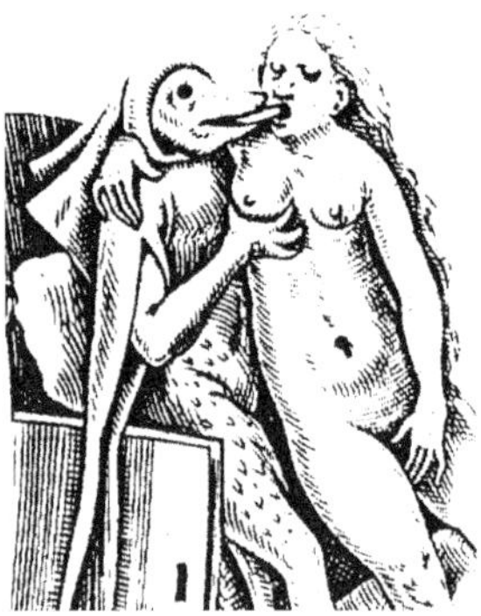

25

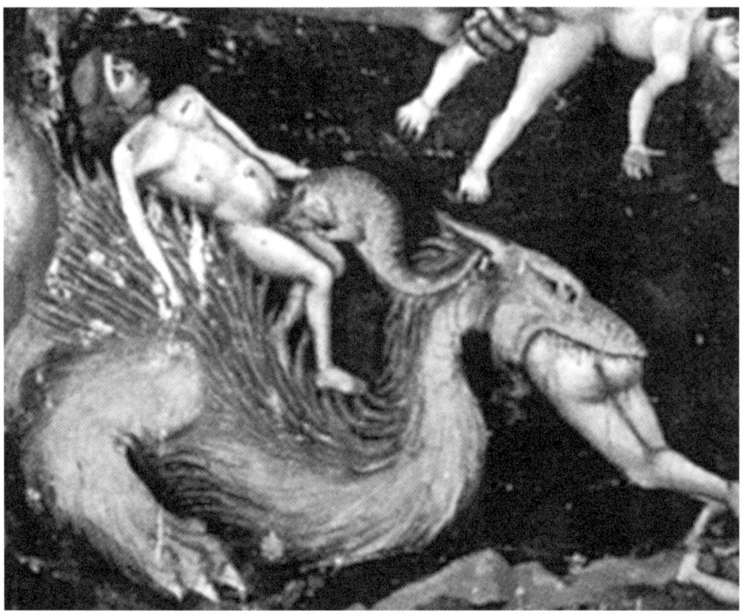

The anxiety of being castrated
by a devouring sexual organ
was translated
into patriarchal imagery
through monsters
being contiguous to women,
submitting them
to lustful acts or
worse torments.

Iconographies of the female sex

Generally, iconographies of the female sexual organs turn out to be much more scattered, much more bizarre than those of the male sexual organ, which, in any case, have been the subject of general knowledge books. For that reason they are often stamped with a highly revealing and instructive value about the place allocated to women throughout history and civilizations. The representations of her sexual organs, from a chronological point of view, disclose first the cult devoted to them, their identification with the divine entrance, or, on a lesser level, an apology with regard to their reproductive function. Secondly, what these iconographies reveal is no less than the agitation of all those considerations, with the progressive establishing of the patriarchal order, combined with the apparition of male gods in the Greek Pantheon. Despite a few isolated sexual mysticisms that attribute to the female sexual organs a more or less equivalent vocation to that of man towards the cosmogony, they were hidden and vilified with the coming of monotheist religions, notably Judeo-Christianity. That has been translated through representations corresponding to the dirty, but, above all, bestial aspect of female "nature" which has to be tamed or fought. And when, finally, artists showed the female sexual organs freed from their phobic conceptions and in a more opportune light, other dangers appeared which also contributed to discredit them. Today we are far from the glorification which prevailed in prehistoric times and which history cunningly undertook to silence.

Sacralization of the female

Only in the Twentieth Century have many small statuettes been discovered, primarily female, morphologically very different, sometimes inscribed with rhomboidal shapes that evoke the female sexual organs. More rudimentary female representations have been found too, vulvae carved on rock faces or symbolized by terracotta triangles, or pendeloques, circular pendants embellished with a seed. These different pieces can reflect diverse explanatory accounts. They could be lucky charms or objects linked to the social status of women: archetypes of femininity and its functions which would underline the fertile side of the female being, its regenerative power. They could also be representations linked to the sphere of the sacred, representations of plural divinities, or different expressions of the same deity, a universal Mother Goddess. Several propositions exist regarding the belief in a simple Great Mother creator of the world, a benevolent and positive spirit, assuring the prosperity of flourishing paleoagrarian societies. The possibility of that very ancient cult lasted perhaps several millennium, affected probably the major part of Europe, if not Eastern Europe, since many statuettes endowed with a hole or a slit in their lower part, or characterized by the presence of a pubic triangle, have been found in Russia and Siberia.

The Neolithic period also seems concerned with the hypothesis of that religious tribute given to one or more female divinities. Numerous statuettes dating from that period have been discovered in Asia (Syria, Iraq, Iran, etc). Those figurines are seated, inscribed in a triangle, or, in a more rudimentary way, they are hyperschematized productions reduced to incised pebbles, some notably from Palestine. Stone and terracota idols have been found too, their sexual organs conceptualized by an exaggerated pubic triangle, or expressed by the position of their legs. Also, those statuettes sometimes rest against wild beasts, likely to be perceived as symbols of power, wisdom and divine energy. Several interpretations question this concept of Mother Goddess and prefer to follow the line of a representation of the mother as being at the origin of

Slowly they turned into
hideous creatures
inspired by
the most irrepressible
mythical figures such as the
Lamies, Harpies,
Melusines, etc.

26

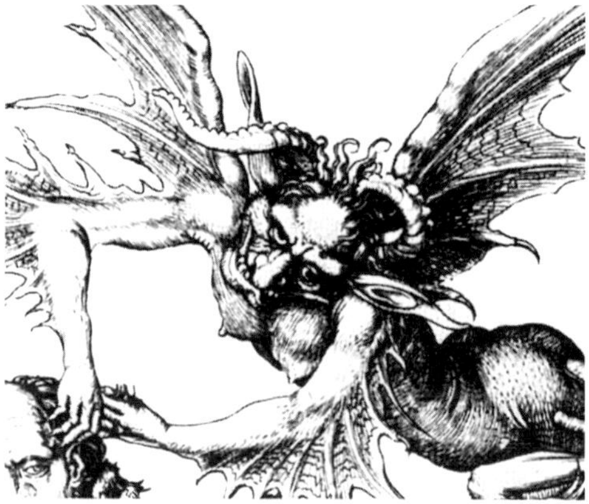

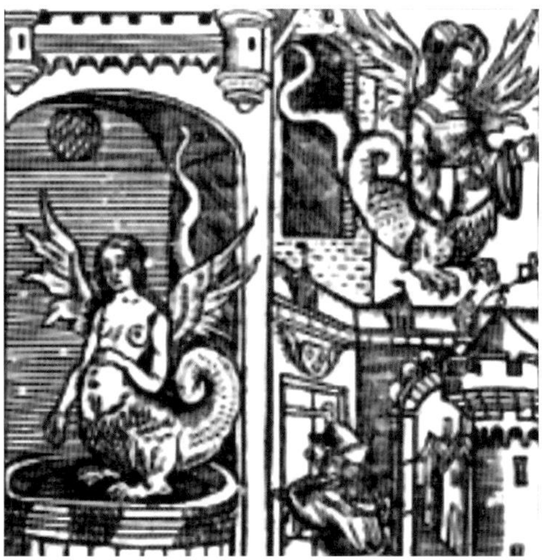

27

a lineage. It would therefore be thanks to a distant ancestor that the family existed. Her fat body would result from successive pregnancies, from the whole family she has given birth to and would continue to give birth to for many generations. It would be a permanent founder, outside time and, in a certain manner, immortal.

Whatever one's favourite hypothesis, it remains a fact that the figurines became rarer after the third millennium. They were often found represented in a childbirth position, which tended to prove that women were particularly praised as biological actors of reproduction. After that, from the Bronze Age and through the second millennium, representations of birth disappeared and the universal idea as the genetrix waned gradually. That decline announced a social change that seemed propitious to promote and establish a certain male power.

The weakening of the female hegemony

Throughout antiquity, particularly in Greece, this male power was expressed by the emergence of an entire pantheon of gods who arrived on the scene to compete with their female congeners. The idea of a Great Deity emerging in prehistoric times divided into a series of specific goddesses who were generally subordinate to the male gods. The representations that have been made of them were very significant in the change in the status of women. While the god's nudity and his sexual (even reduced) attributes had a part in his sacred nature, the goddess was often draped in cloth. This can be verified, for example, in the given representations of Apollo or Aphrodite – though she would have been masculinized since, according to Marie Delcourt[1], the image of a bearded Aphrodite with the body and clothes of a woman, but a beard and ithyphallic sexual organ, would have been venerated in Cyprus. Goddesses were generally dressed in light and tight-fitting clothes, what

[1] Marie Delcourt, *Hermaphrodite. Mythes et rites de la Bisexualité dans l'antiquité classique*, P.U.F, Paris, 1958, pp. 46, 47.

French people call the "draperie mouillée" (wet look). These would serve the mood of temperate sensuality and decency henceforth carried forward in what concerned women. Her nudity was rarely represented in the great period of Greek Art. Women could be found on attic vases dating from the Sixth Century BC, but they had no elegance or grace, which was somewhat quashed during the Fifth Century BC. In that period the sexual organs were omitted, for example in sculpture, where the space was filled with a "monticule de saindoux" (monticule of lard), to employ terms of French naturalist writers. But that omission was not necessarily sufficient to respect the decency of the time. So the Venuses often had a hand modestly covering their sexual organs (which, in any case, "didn't exist"), such as the Venus of Cnidus, made by Praxiteles, which dated from around 350 BC.

Gradually, the theme of Venus in the Hellenistic period, at the beginning of the Roman period, passed from the domain of religion to entertainment and ornamentation, then ended by disappearing. Nevertheless, popular erotic mosaics and paintings, including the female nude, could be found, for example, in Pompei.

The resurgences of female power

We need to leave the Western frame to find once more the eroticized representations of female divinities. In Ancient Egypt, where the image of the ithyphallic phallus inherent to the god prevailed, the goddess Hathor (goddess of love and joy, but also of death and a new becoming) was not naked in her representations, but often endowed with the *menit*[2]. In the stylized form of that sacred object could be glimpsed the image of the female sexual organs, all the better because it was Hathor who prompted the liberation of the creative forces of the God Atum by masturbation or expectoration.

[2] Sacred object of Hathor, the *menit* represented, in a very stylized way, the erotic female lures: abundant hair, breasts and sexual organs.

28

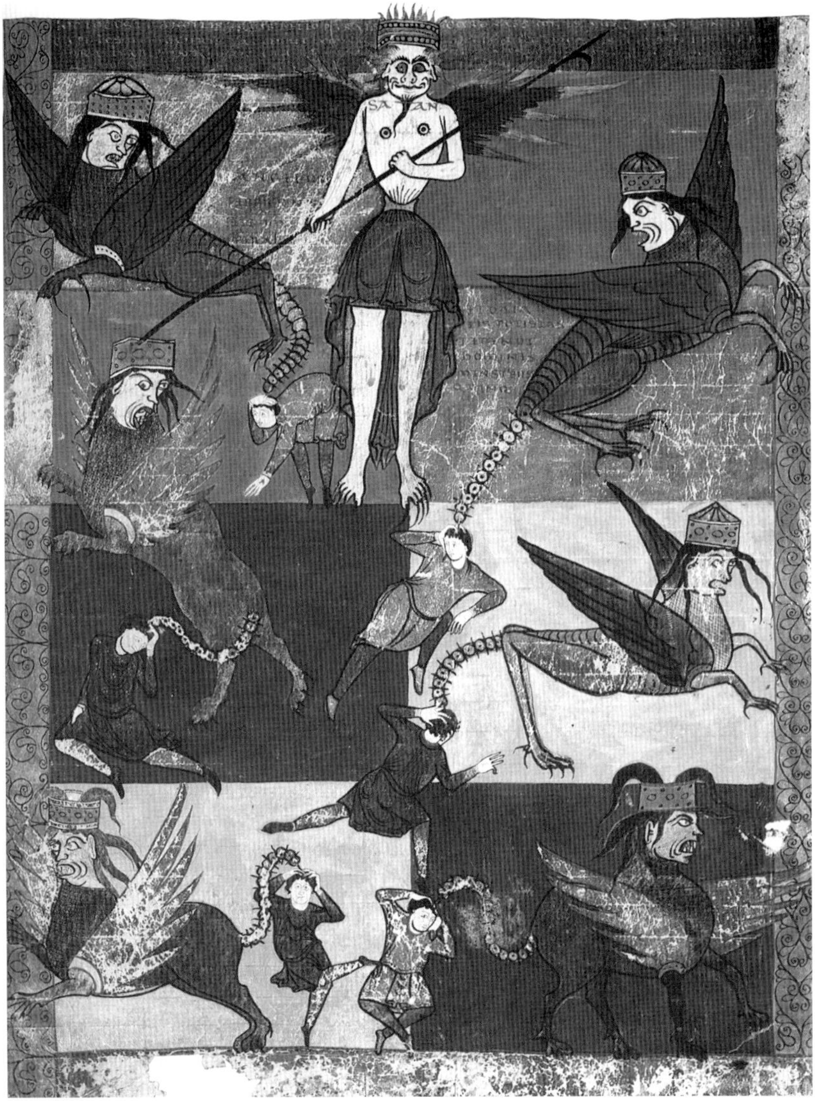

Their unrivalled ugliness and sordid deformity
were in reality the personification of absolute Evil, entrusted to impress
or scare the last defenders of paganism, to literally reach the spirits...

This idea of female involvement towards the creation was found, on a minor scale, on the Asian Continent, more precisely in China, around the First Century of our Christian era. Taoism, which developed at the beginning of the Imperial era (Second Century BC), rested on the belief in a double cosmic force which would be both male and female at the same time, as well as generated the whole universe and animated everything it contained. We knew all these *yin* and *yang* energies: the *yin* energy incarnated the dark, terrestrial and female force, while the *yang* energy incarnated the luminous, celestial and male force. Those energies, dualist, but also complementary, interacted with each other inside the macrocosmic life. And man, in general, considered as a microcosm, was also marked with those *yin-yang* energies. The originality of Taoism was to propose that the man harmonized those fluctuating movements in order to transcend the apparent possibilities of his true nature and perpetuate it by the use of coitus that, thus, became highly sacred and magical. In that context, the sexual organs were obviously glorified. So, to designate the vulva, the Chinese language used the phrase "door of jade". It also referred to it by the name of a precious red-coloured mineral, the cinnabar. From an iconographic point of view, everything was more complex because everything had disappeared. One could only base one's argument on the copies which dated from the Ming dynasty (1570-1644), which were given for originals of the previous eras (T'ang and Song: 618-1279). On them one could see female characters exposing their nudity entirely and copulating with men. Their sex was at the centre of Taoist disciplines. Its *yin* essence (her uterine and vaginal secretions) was awakened by foreplay in the sexual act, like cunnilingus, in order to increase and reinforce the *yang* essence of the man (his spermatic fluid). So, the man, after having sojourned judiciously in the "fountain of jade" (the vagina) of spouses, concubines and prostitutes could hope to reach a state of blissfulness leading to his perpetuation. As for the woman, she would secure a uterine ground propitious to the conception of healthy male offspring. Let's say it's something of a chauvinistic view.

This taoist discipline closely resembled occult tantric disciplines, being particular forms of Hinduism, Buddhism and Jainism. These disciplines developed in India, Tibet, in the Indochinese peninsula, China and Japan as early as the First Century of the Christian era and are still alive today. They profess the mode by which man could re-animate and take control of the celestial forces he concealed in himself in order to reach a state of transcendence and that, particularly, through the use of sexual practises. Those sacred practises were synonymous with the Divine Couple (which materialized the union between the male and female principles), being at the origin of the world. So, we find on the one hand a large iconography underlying the teachings of sacred texts (*tantra*) which showed various magico-ritual positions of embrace, some particularly difficult for women to have to adopt in order to promote the conditions of a sustained pleasure. On the other hand, there existed numerous tantric representations dedicated to the cult of the god (Shiva) and the goddess (Shakti) which were, anyway, One in the Absolute. They were generally represented in a carnal union characterized by the immobility of the god, while the goddess performed all the love-making movements. That female sexual dynamism (generally conferred on the man in western society) was due to the fact that the goddess was the cosmic energy, nature's energy, while the god represented its immutable aspect. Without her, Shiva would remain not dead as such, but inert, inactive, inefficient. Shakti was the creative energy of Shiva, the energy of his divine semen. In a way she was the one who set his sperm in motion (that idea was carried out on ritual sexual practises by the priority given to the woman's actions, which were supposed to favour the elevation of the man towards the absolute). Her importance was such that she was often represented alone, standing up, with redundant limbs or lying on her back, legs spread wide. Sometimes her sexual organs only were reproduced, sometimes with an added phallus in their centre. As a general rule, the sexual part of the Divine Mother sufficed to symbolize universal creation, but the followers never forgot that it was impregnated with the male fertilizing principle. In a sense, the diagrams (*yantra*) which were used in meditation mixed the schematization of the goddess's pubis (a triangle with the point downwards) with that of the god's penis (a triangle with the point upwards). One could see their imbrication in the designs on the ground in Indian temples. The sacred formulae of tantrism (*mantra*) also sometimes formed a rosary in the shape of a vulva, which here too was penetrated by the fertilizing principle of the god. But as creation led inevitably to death and destruction, the goddess could also take on a frightening appearance that was nothing more than the other side of the resplendent one she presented. She was called then Kalî, Durgâ, Lakshmi, Ganesha, etc. She was painted black, held a sword in her hand, wore a necklace made of fifty severed heads, positioned herself on the motionless body of the god, either a few centimetres from his erect penis or copulating with him. Her neck too could be severed. It was associated with her sexual organs for magic and fluidic energies flowed from it, which had the appearance of menstruation. There was no question here of the killing of the female or of the evocation of the castrating woman (if one considered beheading as a symbolic transfer of castration). On the contrary, tantric texts called the menstrual blood, the "nutritious blood", so beneficial and fertilizing was it supposed to be. This point of view urged some followers to copulate with menstruating women in order to transcend their conditioned state and to access more securely a state of absolute being. It was evident that this acceptance remained entirely singular, for those practices were commonly condemned, for menstrual flow was charged with a highly negative and disturbing aspect… a point I will develop later.

Occultation and disdain towards the female

Outside of these sexual mysticisms, which only involved a faithful minority, the woman was no longer deified. In the Judeo-Christian religion everything started badly for her, everything was devoted to erase from history the memory of the prehistoric Great Goddess. First, there was Lilith, Adam's first wife according to Kabbalistic tradition, who was flung into the abyss, into a world of vice, depravity and dark pulsions as

29

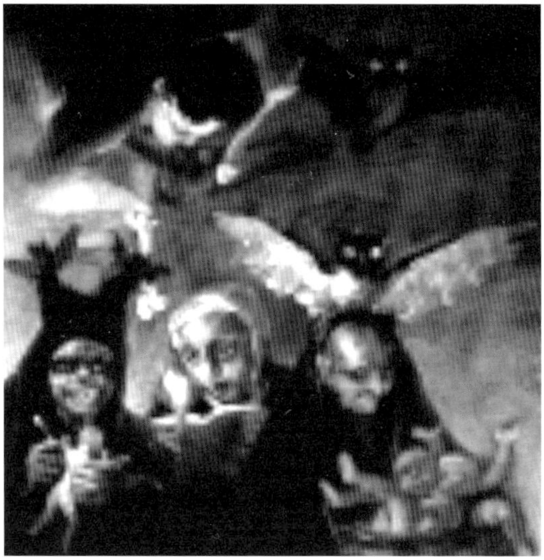

The owl too
could be allied to woman
to signify
her ghoulish belonging
to chthonic forces.

All these lustful monsters,
that were supposed to express
the perverse instincts of women,
were only reflections of
the demonized figure of Lilith,
often represented as an owl
that had also become a bad-omen,
although in the past it symbolized
a thoughtful animal
whose wise and meditative gaze
was able to see in the dark.

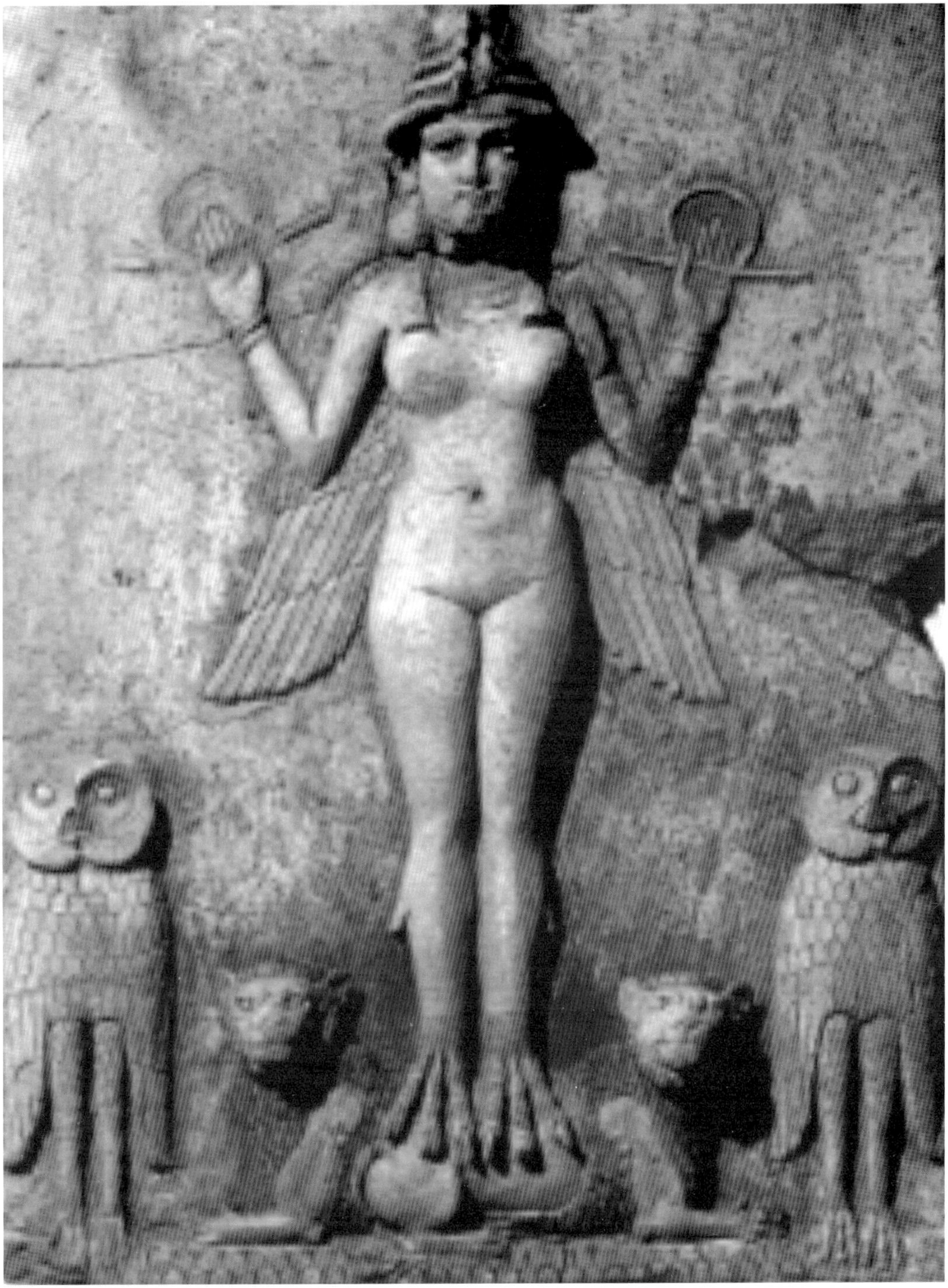

she didn't agree to be submissive, dominated and thus rebelled. She was replaced by Eve, the second to be created, who had to be the obedient assistant of Adam, her spouse. But as a deliberate act, she committed the fatal sin, she succumbed to temptation and corrupted the man by tempting him. Thus she deserved to be responsible for human tragedy, to be considered as weak, seductive, dangerous too, and in her turn to suffer God's judgement on her sexual organs (which I'll return to later). The Virgin Mary was the only one capable of redeeming somehow the image of the woman in the patristic tradition, to counterbalance the image of the Evil woman. But the task was hard, particularly as it was her virginity that was the supreme value and, consequently, its loss was negatively perceived even in marriage. There were indeed a few representations that tried to go against that supreme virginity by putting forward the image of maternity. By doing so they gave the Virgin Mary a privileged character. Thus, in the Middle Ages, many statuettes represented her pregnant and included a belly which was sometimes detachable and contained the images of the Trinity. In an illumination (made in 1490 in the Pinturicchio workshop) the Virgin Mary took the place of God the Father's body while she carried the infant Jesus in her womb.

Without resorting to her image, other representations of esoteric characters tried to re-establish the divine harmony between male and female. Some (like the one made by Hildegarde de Bingen in 1150) referred to the old cosmogonic symbol of the egg, its germinative richness as the Principle of things and evoked in that the female sexual organs. Others were more astonishing. For example, an illumination made by Bonne de Luxembourg in 1345 drew Christ's wound as a diamond shape. That wound was then unexpectedly feminized, to such an extent that it appeared as a vulva.

The chain to contempt

Except for those few scattered iconographies, priority was given to God the Father and his son at the expense of the female, who not only

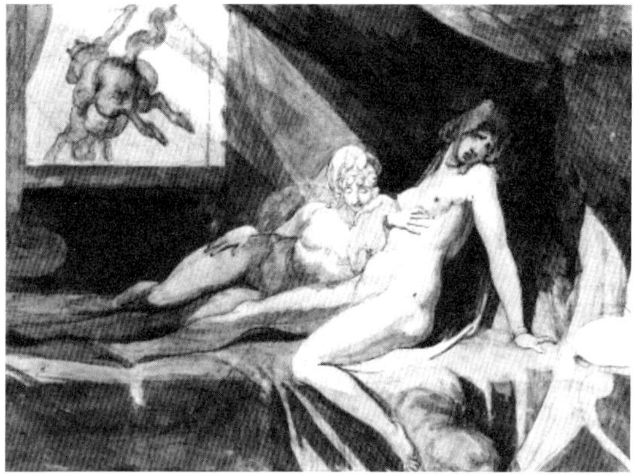

32

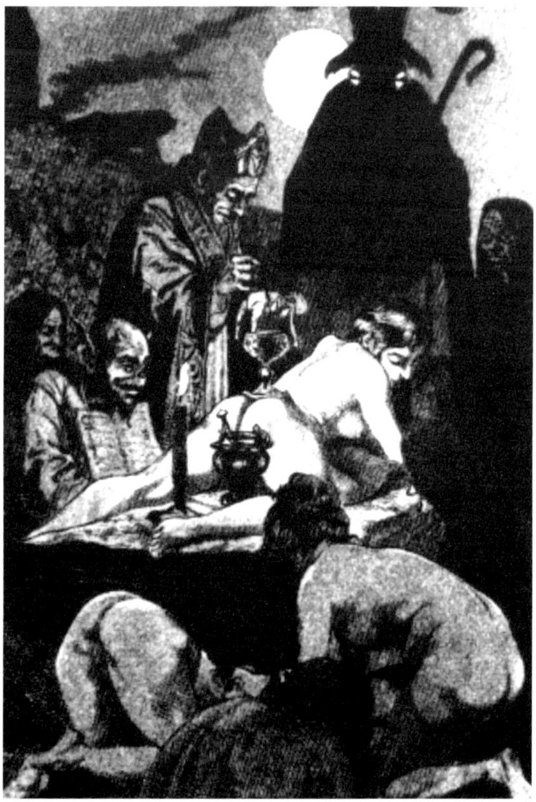

31

From that point on women were seen
coupling with the devil
who then became
one of her succubi.
For that reason women were
the devil's accomplices
and their favourite agents.

was going to be hidden, but moreover was going to be vilified. So in many Roman churches one found vulgar and hostile caricatures of women who were Evil incarnated. They were there to restrain the congregation, to warn them against the libidinous and dangerous nature of all Eve's daughters. They generally appeared in degrading positions and exhibited their "vaginal hole" in which was frequently inserted the fingers of their hand(s). Likewise other female characters indicated their sex with their left hand. That despised left hand was also used for the intimate washing of the anus after each defecation; it channels the fecal matter considered as being abject and contaminated for the man. Applied to the female crutch, the left hand revealed the amalgam which was made between the anal and genital zone (and their extensions : menstrual and birth blood, cervical glair, etc). It bore witness to that imbroglio. Besides, today still, slang classes the vulva with the behind, in other words calls the vulva "cul" (ass)*. That mixture of vulva-ass echoes the animal cloaca, the common orifice that many birds, reptiles, fish and amphibians possess and which serves to evacuate their excrements and urine as well as for genital usage. On that, in 1905, Sigmund Freud footnoted in his book *Three essays on the Theory of Sexuality* that "the clear-cut distinction between anal and genital processes which is later insisted upon is contradicted by the close anatomical and functional analogies and relations which hold between them. The genital apparatus remains the neighbour of the cloaca, and actually in the case of women is only taken from it on lease."[3] I'd like to remind you here that the Latin etymology of the word cloaca (*cloaca-ae*) means drains.

Following that comparison, women's sexual organs are dirty, spoilt, foul; what Mathias Neithart dit Grunewald illustrated, in *Les amants*

* In English there is no similar confusion, as in French with "cul," the word ass (U.S.) (or arse in U.K.) very specifically referring to the buttocks. However, there is confusion with the word "fanny", in that the United States uses the word "fanny" as a specific "buttocks" reference, whereas "fanny" as used in Britain refers to the vulva. Though today the British are so used to American film and television references to the word "fanny" as to no longer raise an eyebrow. (Trans.)

[3] Sigmund Freud, *Three essays on the Theory of Sexuality* (1905) in *On Sexuality*, Vol 7 of the Pelican Freud Library, Penguin Books, London, 1977, p.104.

That was how a sexual monster of a new genre was born:
the witch who, thanks to her good looks and cravings,
could lead anyone to the abyss of her sensuality,
in other words, into hell.

33

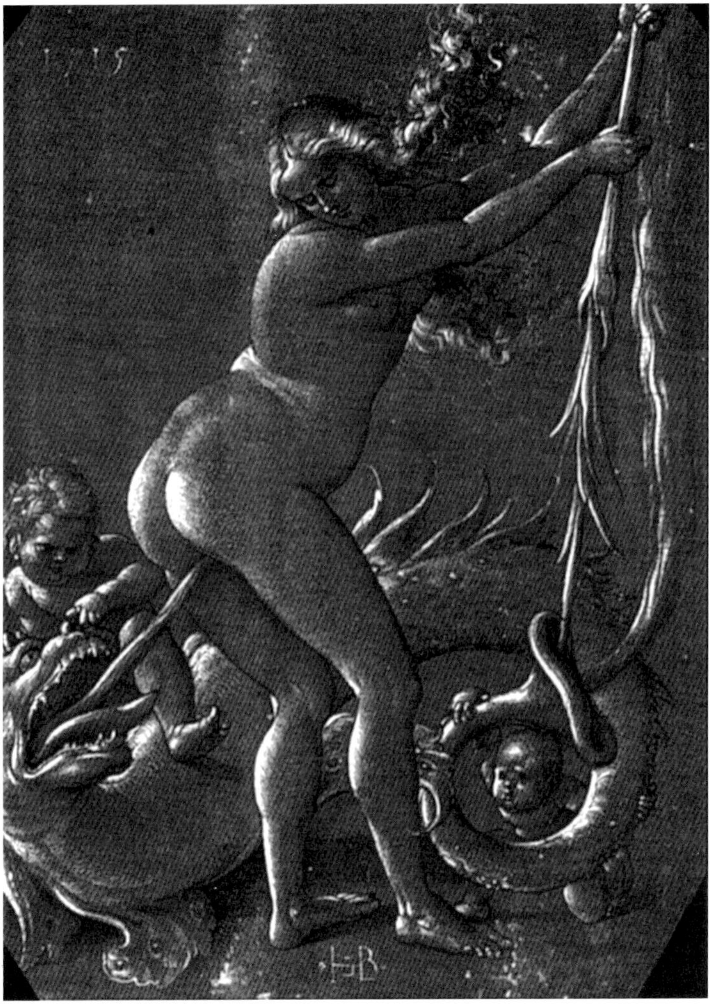

34

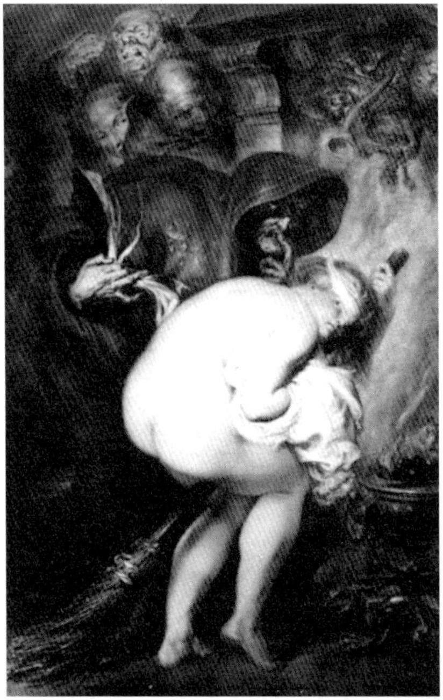

36

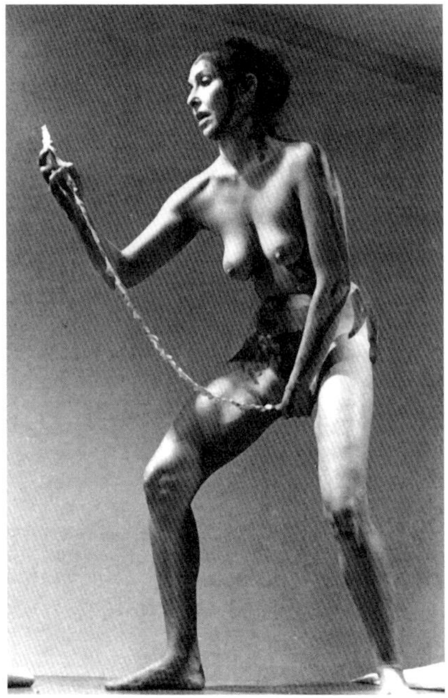

35

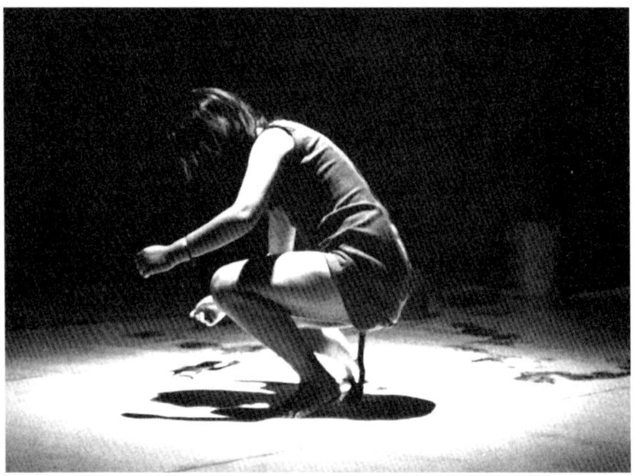

The broom with which they were rigged out
appeared as a highly suggestive accessory,
especially because of the position of the fingers grasping it,
which one can see here as ironically diverted...

trépassés (1490) with a toad stuck on it, attracting flies. However, the female sex also concerned many other animal metaphors. Its "nature" became the thing with a beasty name; for example, *choïros* in Greek means both the vulva and piglet. But it was especially the hairiness of the sex that was responsible for so many animal names. It goes, of course, from cat or kitten to rabbit, hedgehog, monkey, sheep, etc. Even the depilated sexual organs of women were called "skinned bitch" by Aristophanes. Its odour too was as strong as that of animals. Talking of which, surely, there is both "putois" (skunk) thus "puant" (stinking) and "puits" (well) in the word "putain" (whore).

The dangerous sexual lair

That idea of well goes with the other names given to the vulva. One often hears about the fault, breach, slit and other terms that revert back to the notion of danger (the abyss, the cut), but also to the notion of defense (in battle, one says, "to be on the breach," "to batter a breach," and the slit can also imply the action of slitting). The danger towards the female sexual organs often translated into the universal toothed vagina myth. Hundreds existed, where the question was to destroy those vaginal or vulvar teeth with sticks, metallic bars or big pebbles forced into the sexual orifice to break them. At other times, it was rather the rule to extract them with the help of strings or pincers. That castrating vagina-jaw was found in diverse representations, even in the Twentieth Century, for it was painted literally by Roberto Matta (in *La femme affamée*, *Rêve ou morte*), or tied to *l'Araignée* (the Spider) which captured its lovers in the threads of its vulvar web for Alfred Kubin. The idea of vagina-jaw also emanated from some carnivorous flowers (as *Cajophora latérita*) that Karl Blossfeld photographed or bivalve shells which crushed those who dared to venture inside them (in Jérôme Bosch's *Delights triptych*, the mussel contained two human bodies whose lower limbs only showed).

In order to reveal the dangerous side of the female sexual organs, other myths proposed starving eels which crawled inside the vaginal cavity (in Polynesia), or else snakes (in Bulgarian, Serbian, Russian, Siberian and other folklore). One could also find snakes in the mythological figure of the Medusa that surrounded her "vaginal mouth" fitted with teeth, as in Caravaggio's representation. Her snake-hair could, effectively, evoke pubic hair. As for Sigmund Freud, he interpreted them as "a multiplication of penis symbols"[4] supposed to diminish or challenge the risk of castration linked to the Medusa figure. This interpretation went hand in hand with the disparagement he usually showed towards the female sexual organs. He didn't cease in his work to note the horror and fright provoked by the vision of the woman's genitals. In fact, it seemed that he wanted to dissipate that feeling of repulsion, disgust and dread by projecting the penis on the female sexual organs (establishing as a general rule a phallic perception of the female, with her desire to possess a penis like the male). But by putting forward the reality of the male sexual organ and erasing that of the female, Freud didn't do anything more than reiterate the domination exercised by the patriarchal power over women, to cover up for its phantasmal power. He reminded us of the "castration" carried out by men on women, and put forward that fear of being castrated as felt by the man was connected to the thought that women could take revenge on that initial act by reproducing it. In fact that fear was typically male and at the origin of the toothed vagina myth; the idea of the castrating penis didn't exist, with a few exceptions.

Finally, if the snakes that were mixed with the myth of the toothed vagina echoed the phallus, they especially echoed its predominance. And far from weakening the fear of castration that was connected with Medusa, they rather seemed to reinforce that committed on her by Perseus. For the beheading carried out by the Greek hero was a symbolic transfer of castration. So, the severed neck was nothing else but the emblem (symbol) of a sexual organ which was no more than cut and

[4] Sigmund Freud, "Medusa's Head" (1922) in *Sexuality and the Psychology of Love*, Collier, New York, 1963, p.212.

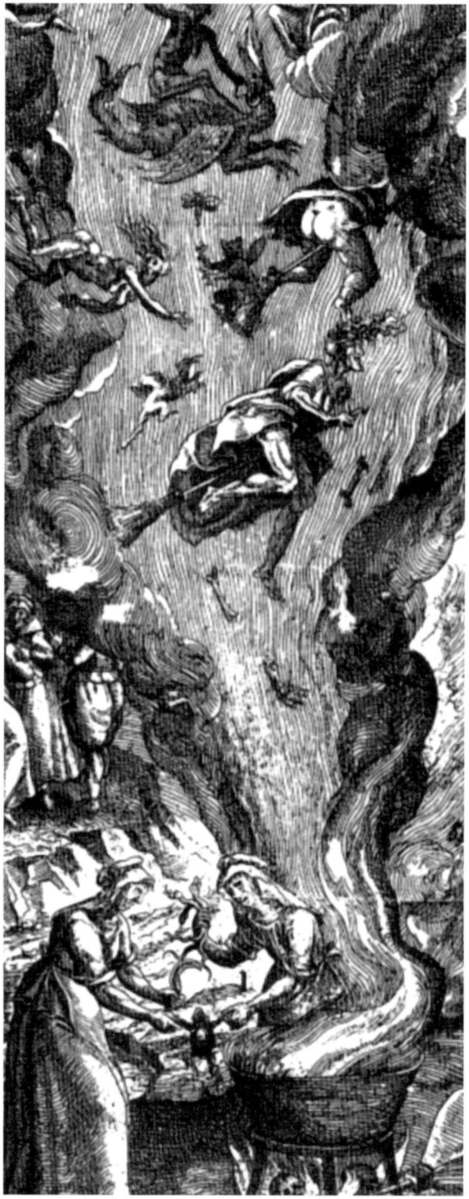

Witches were given a cauldron that contributed to their maleficent powers: to precipitate anyone into eternal damnation and to spread evils such as weather incidents harmful to harvests, or fires, epidemics, sterility...

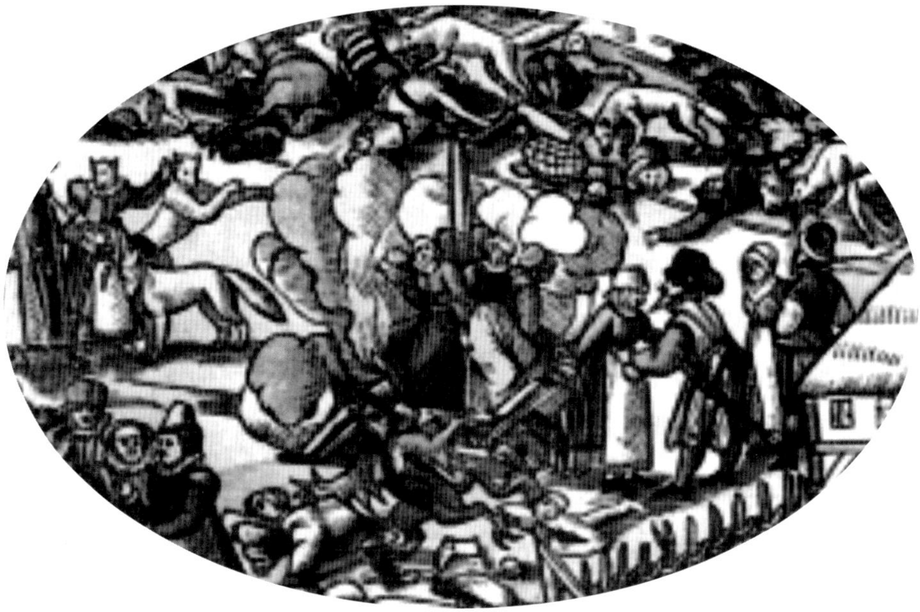

All the negative powers attributed to women designated them as scapegoats for the Inquisitions and augured the numerous bonfires they would feed.

separated, a sex brought back to reason[5], won over by the phallocratic order.

This interpretation found an echo in the association of the snake with Eve, according to the Old Testament. The intervention of the snake was first going to disparage and degrade women, then to incriminate them, to make them responsible in a way for the original sin; and, finally, it was going to trigger off menstruation and determine various gynecological consequences: suffering in pregnancy, pain in childbirth. That causality was attested by many iconographic documents (from the Asian Neolithic to the American Indian cultures) where circular shapes symbolizing the womb or diamond shape echoing the vulva were added to the body of the animal[6]. According to certain myths too, the snake, attracted to the woman, would have bitten her sexual organs, and periods would have started. In some Roman churches, that link was literally translated by the representation of a snake disappearing up a woman's vagina, if not into her breast. It is interesting here to mention the phrase "to nourish a snake in one's breast" which means protecting someone who wants to harm you. That formula confirmed the idea that the woman was in a way the accomplice of the reptile, that she participated in the evil effect it had on her person. She encouraged the intrusion of the snake in her existence, its sexual impact and the harm that resulted. Therefore she was proven to be in a certain way responsible for the evil which had introduced itself into the world by using her sexual organs.

5 "[...] to behead is to bring back to reason." J. Clair, *Méduse, contribution à une anthropologie des arts du visuel*, Gallimard, Paris, p. 142 (the author refers to the words of M. Griaule, in *Dieu d'eau*).

6. In most iconographies, the snake associated with the womb was not marked with the negative significance that Judeo-Christianity was only too willing to hold against it. It rather manifested itself as a symbol of temporal transformation: on the one hand, it was an animal endowed with the faculty of rejuvenation (it mutated), and on the other, it was linked, in several cultures, to the lunar cycle (it disappeared and reappeared at the same rhythm as the moon and was said to have as many coils as the moon cycle had days). That closeness, in the link between menstrual cycle and moon, conferred on the snake a feminoid aspect and opened up on the other system of symbols it covered: that of fecundity. In that sense, countless myths compared the snake to the yin principle of prolific humidity, while others compared it to the great carrier of semen (for with its oblong shape it recalled a penis).

The curse of menstruation

The blood of menstruation is symptomatic of that evil; it is dangerous because it is the first clock synchronized with the lunar cycle: it results from time passing and augurs death. It is truly a malediction, it takes on a negative and disturbing aspect which sullies the female sexual organs a little bit more. I think about *Train* (1993), Kiki Smith's work, displaying a naked woman who drags behind her snaking strings of red beads trickling from her vulva and appertaining, obviously, to menstrual blood. By showing it, the artist goes against one of the most virulent taboos, when one knows that menstrual blood, like birth blood, is more impure than blood from murder[7]. It is the indication of a dangerous complicity that women maintain with terrifying forces. It incarnates "the dread which doesn't let itself be represented or signified, which doesn't accede to the scene and remains radically ob-scene"[8]. Universally, men have applied themselves to cut it out, to exorcize it, to exclude it from sight. The Léviticus (XV, 19) and the Koran (II, 222) express the horror inspired by the woman menstruating, likewise the Vedas, the laws of Manou, etc. In Mali, the Dogon people believe a man will die if he catches sight of menstrual or birth blood.

A multitude of purification rites exist that are destined to counter-act and conjure the malignancy of menses. They rely in reality on washing, on isolating women, on putting them in quarantine after giving birth and on prohibiting them from touching anything in case they spoil it, implying that a woman having her period makes wine turn sour, milk go off, meat putrefy, salting go bad, honey and fruits rot, and that even her gaze tarnishes mirrors or corrodes metals. To not submit to them represents as much threats of illness and death. Nowadays in Europe a menstruating woman still risks "making mayonnaise curdle", according to popular belief. Even the ads for pads and tampons use a blue liquid, an immaterial and pure colour, to demonstrate their capacity for absorption.

[7] Jean Paul Roux, *Le Sang, Mythes et Réalités*, Fayard, 1988, p. 100.

[8] Daniel Bougnoux, *Terreur et Représentation*, Ellug, Université Stendhal, Grenoble, 1996, p. 308.

41

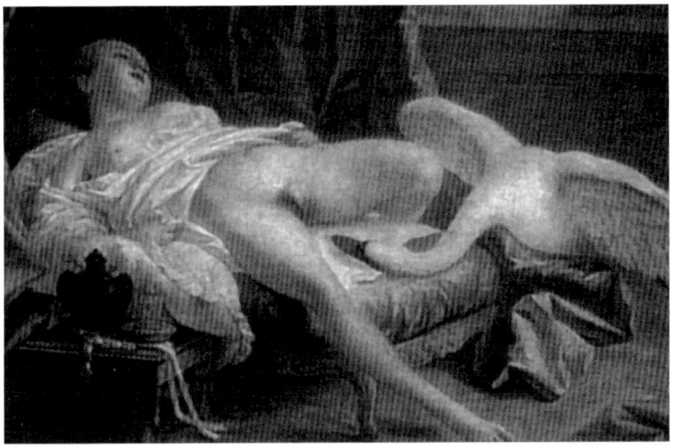

39

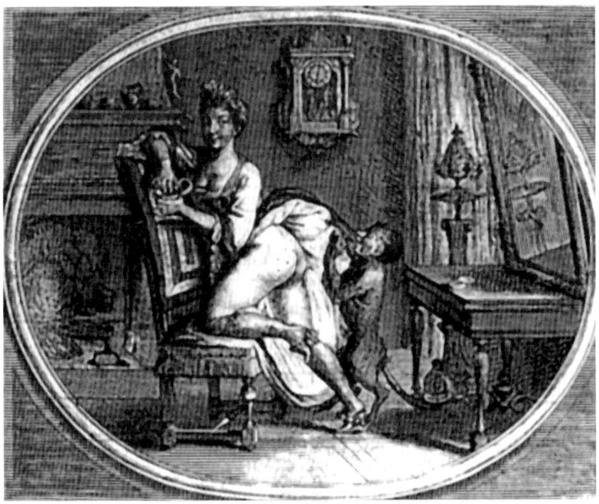

40

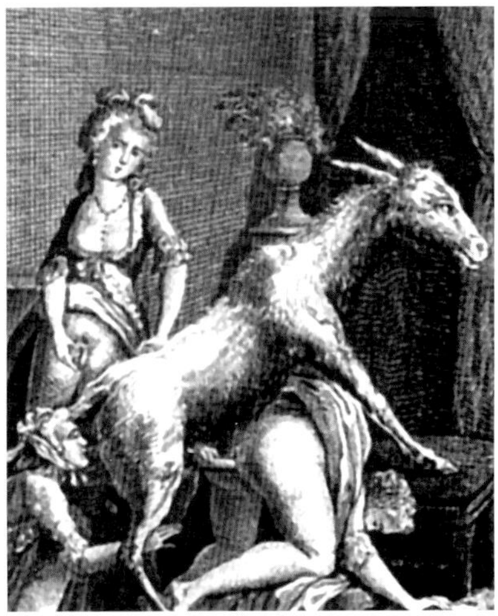

Erotic imagery took over
that of sexual depravity associated with witches
and underlined the perverse and extreme eroticism
generated by the neurosis of a whole era.

Once again it is necessary to conjure the bad omen, which means obscenity, which is connected to the suggestion of menstrual blood; to palliate that bloody provocation of the female "nature" which only results in intensifying the pathological fragility of an organ both humid and plunged into darkness.

In Africa, notably, practises of extraction destined to remove the "evil" of sexual organs exist, and coexist with a circumcision that's supposed to release man from the birth blood. The excision: the removal of the clitoris and small labia can be completed with infibulation: the section of big labia and their quasi-complete junction. The sexual organs almost disappear, and sexual pleasure is totally annihilated (cf Cathy de Monchaux, *Dangerous Fragility*, 1994). It would perhaps be more correct to talk about the "animal pleasure" of women, about their state of nature, that one has to short-circuit in order to subdue it better. Anyway, female jouissance seems detached from obvious procreative virtue. Women can be pregnant without having had an orgasm, contrary to men's jouissance that by definition coincides with the emission of generative semen.

The machination of religious and state authorities

This radical denial of women's pleasure, and thus of their desire, expressed itself by much craftier ways in our western societies. Everything was done to signify women's formidable animal instinct, the dangerous nature of females, and to push people to be on their guard against it. Women were looked at as monsters of desire, in a literal sense. Rather than sexual organs, she was provided with a fish tail (especially in Roman Art); she was metamorphosed into a siren symbolizing the auto-destruction of desire, conjuring up maleficent and formidable Harpies and Erinyes. She was also dressed in a snake tail inspired by Echidna, who was a symbol of the libido which burnt the flesh and devoured it, or of the poisonous tail of a scorpion in some illuminations (*The Apocalypse of St Sever*, made around 1028). In order to perfect it all, to express even

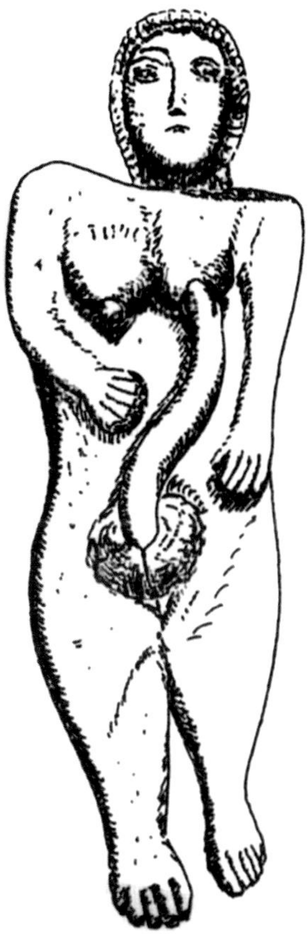

42

43

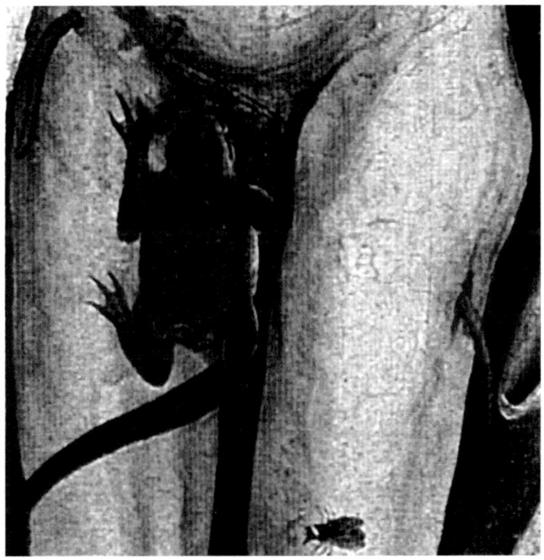

Lust for the female organs
were troubled by a rather disgusting,
even venomous animality.

better women's perverse instincts, they were dressed with the membranous wings of bats in reference to the Lamias, those characters born out of Greek mythology that flew in the air looking for young men whose blood they could suck in order to draw on their vigour. They were also supposed to enter houses in search of small children to devour... One can see here a remanence or a reactualization of the Lilith figure demonized by the patriarchal order, which was going to globally concern women threatening the judicial and symbolic order set up by men. So, the German judiciary corpus dating from the Fifth and Sixth Centuries mentioned the reality of those sinister and cannibalistic women and thus restored a new propensity to the fear they provoked by presuming the devilness of their flesh. Women were no longer simply monstrous, they also took after the devil. This idea was going to re-enforce itself little by little, to such an extent that at the end of the Middle Ages, monstrous and diabolical were going to merge and female characters to be intermixed with them. That would give pictures of creatures often deprived of breasts or with a mouth full of teeth for the lower belly. Several papal bulls in the Thirteenth, Fourteenth and Fifteenth Centuries insisted on the monstrous and diabolical identity of women. They were providers of hell, baits the devil used to attract men. Besides, her sexual organs were compared to a hell mouth, swarming with grinning devils as shown in some Anglo-Norman apocalypses. Sometimes it even contained demonic humors able to provoke different ailments: illnesses, epidemics, male impotence. It was then compared to the witch's cauldron, equivalent to the alchemist vessel. As for the medical thesis, they didn't deny those beliefs and were entirely of the opinion that female sexual organs have a maleficent disposition explained by the attraction caused by its cold, viscous and bloody nature which the devil was only too ready to take hold of. All of that increased enormously the fear of the female and her sexual lair. Finally, we condescended to look at buttocks and sexual organs only to drive out the witches, to discover the obscene mark of the devil, of fornication with him. That could be a red spot, a beauty spot, a scar, a polyp, etc. That godsend, which was the privilege of the inquisitors, was excluded from married life. The body, and, moreover, the sexual organs, represented a dangerous object that we are not allowed to look at or show. Staring at one's spouse was a very serious sin. Bernardin de Sienne quite clearly said: "what has the eye to do with marriage?"[9]

Artistic transpositions and insubordinations

In pictorial representations, nudity appeared in exceptional ways and in very precise conditions, recalling the damnations of the flesh: Adam and Eve during or after the sin, as depicted by Masaccio, Van Eyck, Pol de Limbourg, Lucas Cranach, etc. In these paintings, the female sexual organs were veiled or concealed with an artifact: loincloth, fold, hand. Quite often only the damned women were completely naked; they were wretched and disgraced, as in Bosch and Giotto. The vulva only appeared obscene and repugnant. Therefore man could only repent to succumb to the attraction of what was shown as being desperately ugly. Thus the vulva drawn by Leonardo da Vinci or Jean-Jacques Lequeu.

Even medical drawings only showed diseased and disgusting organs, or organs with something wrong, to which was added a whole gynecological material undeniably aggressive: several forceps that looked like hooks on long handles, hysterolabes, cork-screws for fibroids…, all as if the uterine animal was going to attack and the medical profession had to protect itself against her. I use the word "animal" for, in reality, the uterus has been compared by doctors from antiquity to the end of the Twentieth Century, or almost, to a sea mollusc, an octopus, for, of course, wide open, it does resemble them slightly. In the end, the vision of healthy and pleasant sexual organs remain totally taboo and censured. We prefer to disregard them, to exclude them. The majority of artists erased them (as in the Greco-Roman statues), like Rubens, Raphael, Giorgione,

[9] Bernardin de Sienne, *Prediche volgari* [1427], P. Bargellini, Milan, 1936, t. II, p. 168 (sermon n°21).

Its genital characterization,
mysterious for a long time,
also gave way
to curious
organic dispositions...

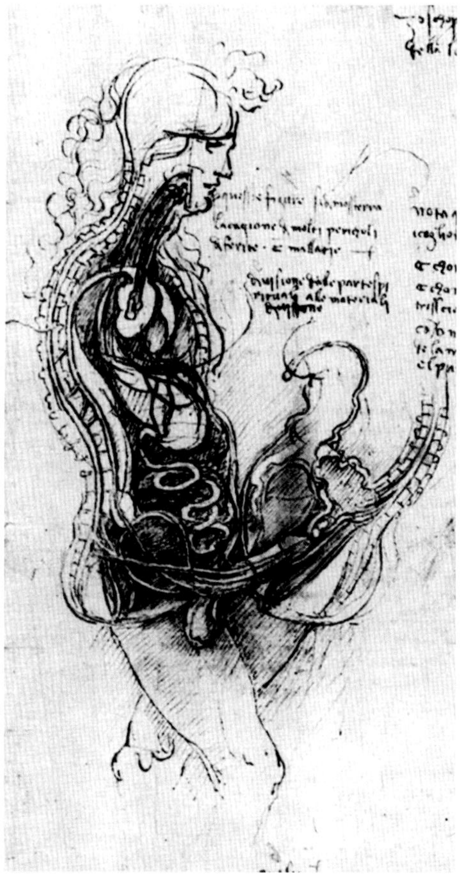

Titien, Bronzino, Jean de Bologne, Ingres, Delacroix, etc. It seemed that censorship was a lot less clerical than the action of the painter or the sculptor, for the image he had of the woman was only a superimposition of inherited representations that, through continuance, appeared natural.

Many years would pass before artists stopped abandoning female sexual organs. Finally, when they re-integrated them into their field of consciousness and suddenly wished to represent them in their authenticity, without omitting their notch, it was undoubtedly with some perversity. When Boucher painted, for example, *Leda and the swan*, that perversity could be zoophilia. Or, on the Richelieu site, in the National Library of France, in what was called "Hell", a great many anonymous drawings and engravings dating from the Sixteenth, Seventeenth and Eighteenth Centuries were seen of an orgiastic and sadistic nature. These perverse scenarios, born from unremitting abstentions of the sin of the flesh, were followed by a plethora of paintings and sculptures where the female was omnipresent. Regarding the obsession with the female that characterized the Nineteenth Century, I would simply recall that when Courbet and Manet applied themselves to represent the reality of the female body and swept aside the conventional cleanliness of erotic codes, they set up the premise for the artistic insubordinations and transformations that followed, to the much more manifest and radical representations of the female sexual organs which were about to be made.

In that way, German artists at the start of the Twentieth Century, passed to a superior degree of monstrosity towards the female genital organs, like Egon Schiele, Otto Dix, George Grosz. Surrealists like Hans Bellmer, André Masson and Victor Brauner did the same in France. But we can't say the representations they all made of the female sexual organs were really glorious. They seemed contradicted by centuries of persecution against the flesh and the lust it generated, they were marked by a phobic or violent subsistence, even if the will of those artists was to give free reign to their desires and show them to the world. They appeared to find it hard to serenely approach the sexual organs without generally adding to them sadistic and degrading fantasies that debased

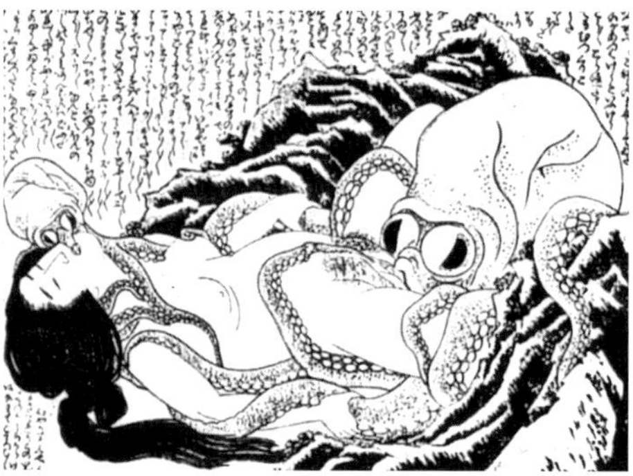

45

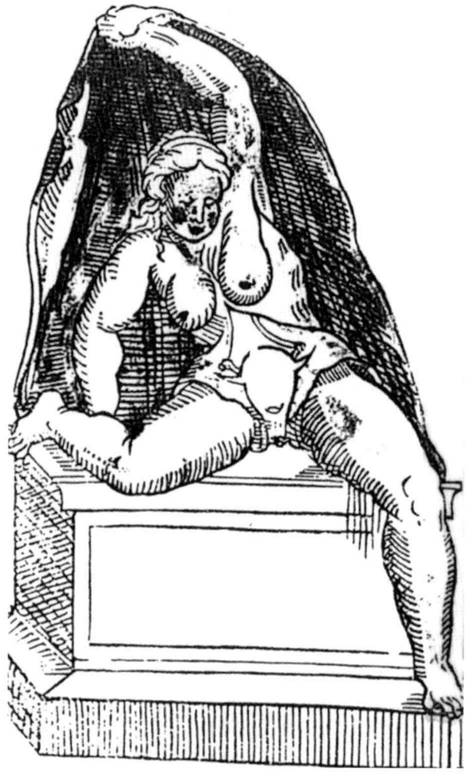

46

Even medical rationality
compared the uterus with the octopus
and associated it with the idea of death,
or at least teratology.

them. Let's not forget that Jean-Paul Sartre expressed his aversion for the female sexual organs in *Being and Nothingness*[10] in 1948 and that Georges Bataille also in Eroticism, 1957, talked about the "hideous animality of the organs", "an object is horrible—or shameful—"[11] to designate them.

The female insurrection

At that time female artists emerged who fought against those perceptions and truly had a reactive, expiatory and cathartic attitude through their art: Virginia Woolf, Meret Oppenheim, Louise Bourgeois, Annette Messager, Valie Export, for example, all tended to bestow on their sexual organs a value equal to that of the penis or at least to give it a new value. The sexual liberation which took over America and Europe in the Sixties and Seventies also revendicated that equality. That equality depended on control over contraceptive devices that allowed women to take power over reproduction (Catholic France was previously under a 1920s law punishing even the mention of contraception). The pill was commercialized in the United States in 1960, in 1967 in France. In 1975 in this country a law was passed which liberalized divorce and in 1979 a law which authorized abortion under certain conditions. *The Hite Report*[12] published in 1976 also gave a new value to the natural capacity of female jouissance, until then assigned to its genetic role of reproduction. This report redefined female sexuality, contradicted Freud's theory on clitoral pleasure considered as the little girl's pleasure and therefore as a hindrance to vaginal pleasure which would give, according to him, a more mature jouissance.

All those laws liberated morals. With *The Hite Report* it removed the guilt from thousands of women, inhibited at the idea of having a

[10] Jean-Paul Sartre, *Being and Nothingness*, Washington Square Press, 1953.
[11] Georges Bataille, *Eroticism*, Calder, London, 1962, & *The Accursed Share*, Zone Books, New York, 1993, p.78.
[12] Shere Hite, *The Hite Report*, Macmillan, New York, 1976.

sexual dysfunctioning (that led at the same time to becoming frigid) and encouraged couples to practice foreplay in order to achieve more successful orgasm, be it vaginal or clitoral. Nevertheless, by conferring on sexual congress the fundamental source of happiness, the sexual revolution has had a perverse effect by diminishing in a different way women's status. Women became vulgarized, commercialized sexual objects. Pornography helped that enormously, for it hypervisualized the female sexual organs, scrutinized them in their smallest details, reduced them to big disproportionate visual blobs brutally extracted from the body's depth to be prostituted. These intensive and abundant exhibitions reduced to nothing, it has to be said, the fears linked to the female genital organs, but they finally made ordinary and mortified all the attraction they contained (as shown in works by Pierre-Yves Gervais, Henri Maccheroni, François Morellet, etc.)

Besides, in the context of the Eighties and Nineties, a certain number of female artists (Helen Chadwick, Carolee Schneeman, Cindy Sherman, Jeanne Dunning, etc) rebelled against those stereotyped and emptied organs, those insipid holes as well as against the desire pushed in an order of production, fructuous, indeed, but mortiferous. I won't dwell on those who, like Catherine Breillat in the cinema, emphasized the female sexual organs by reviving the male behaviour they know so well...

The premises of a new insult

Today it seems that works created by female artists are always placed in a reactive relationship towards their sexual organs and in the compromise of youthness (that cult of values linked to youth). Sylvie Fleury, Rosemarie Trokel, Mariko Mori and Vanesse Beecroft, among others, spontaneously answer through their artistic works this new form of sexist discrimination, for it mainly concerns the ageing signs of women who appear more and more as a redhibotory infirmity. But what is interesting is that they don't only tackle this concept under the angle of numerous aesthetic and therapeutic processes destined to perpetuate health, beauty and sensuality of the body, they also approach it by considering the actual or future biotechnological "progresses", promising to improve all these qualities, to correct or eliminate the faults, and to confer on the body a kind of standardized ideality. Inez van Lamsweerde conceives quasi-synthetic female bodies that are absolutely smooth, hygienic, hairless, sexless, without areolas, without irregularities. What provokes that vision, what we can read implicitly is in reality the risk weighing on the female identity with regard to techniques of medically assisted procreation with which ally (or could ally) the modification of genes, the sexual sorting, the production of embryos using ovaries of embryos or dead bodies, the cloning, the ectogenesis (human gestation outside a human body), etc. Indeed one can see in the spreading of all those interventions (granting to man the possibility to carry out a process that eludes him organically and to master nature), the potential risk to harm even further the female, to dispossess women of their sexual organs, of their free will concerning procreation, in the name of a certain social conception of normality going with the elimination of every physical and moral defect.[13]

Even so, this artist and her sister members maintain, through their works, a defensive attitude towards the threat menacing again and again their sexual organs. They sharply underline the collective difficulty to appreciate the danger of that new form of eugenics which manifested itself in an insidious way in the rise of the biotechnologies, notably in the development of genetic engineering. Doing so they promote the idea of an aesthetic (if not an un-aesthetic) of the obscene, in other words of an art that, caring more about aesthetic codes or the sublimation of our daily realities, shows us the bad omen (according to the prime meaning of the word obscene) of human investigations questioning our nature itself.

[13] The modification of human conception seems well under way if one considers artificial fecundation and insemination, already responsible for a few million conceptions. When those technical reproductions don't remedy the strong probability of a hereditary disease, they meet the fertility crisis which seems to be growing in our societies, to such an extent that it could become major and give us no other possibility than to reproduce by artificial techniques.

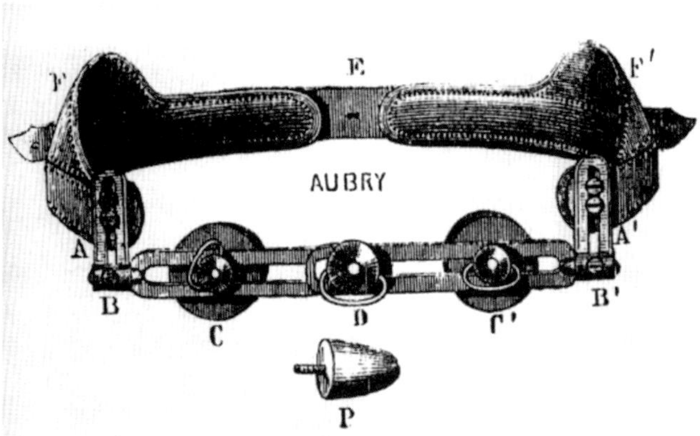

48

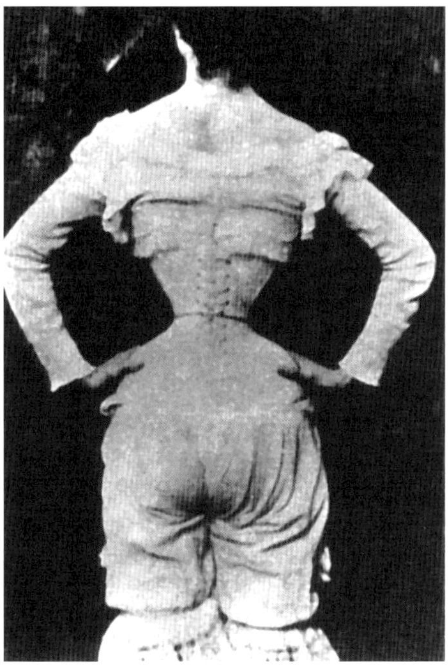

47

Under the pretext of stemming the avidity of the female sexual organs, the drastic measures undertaken by the medical profession in the 19th century went as far as to interfere with the apparatus of seduction.

The Female Sex in Religions

The representation of the female genitals in all forms of art ex-poses (in the etymological sense of the word: places outside) the collective imagination of humankind. Throughout history, its multifarious representations have oscillated between a repulsive, even terrifying realism and a shame-faced erasure with an idealising agenda. Does this mean that artists—women as well as men—find it impossible to look on the female sexual organs in a way that avoids the falsifications of excess? Does it mean that art reflects the ontological status of woman as being still "unspoken"—by herself included—because she is placed in an artificial position of inferiority and subjugation?

An examination of the place of the female genitals within religions—cultural components of society—may cast light on certain secret determinants acting on forms of artistic production over the centuries and even today, when excess is often endorsed by women themselves in the form of an obscenity seen as liberating. Hence my aim of resituating the female sex within religions and rethinking its role. This task, always a difficult one, is both possible and necessary at the start of our new millennium.

Possible because the science of religion, a new discipline which studies the religious phenomenon from its earliest origins and in all its diverse forms, now gives us a methodology and texts which allow the burning question of the status of women within religions to be approached with a maximum of scientific objectivity, taking all religions into account.

Necessary because the sphere of religion cannot be excluded from current challenges to the position of inferiority in which women have been put. Women are now demanding an equal share in political, social, professional and other activities and responsibilities. Can religion be allowed to remain the only human "enterprise" unaffected by the need to bring about equality between men and women?

This possibility and this necessity invite us to explore connections between sex—the female genitalia—and a notion which some have argued is common to all religions: the sacred.

According to the sociologist and ethnologist Marcel Mauss, "it is not the idea of God that is found in all religions, but the idea of the sacred." All religions divide reality into two parts: the profane and the sacred. So it is with the idea of the sacred that we should begin our reflections on the place of women's bodies and the female genitalia in religions.

Sex and the sacred are two words rarely spoken in the same breath, yet, as will become clear, there is between them a hidden similarity which bears out the connection. What is this similarity? Both sex and the sacred harbour forces which are completely out of the ordinary. They share a power which makes them, in the words of the philosopher of religions Rudolf Otto, "*tremendum et fascinans*", terrible and fascinating.

In other words, both possess an extraordinary power which at once frightens and fascinates us. That is undoubtedly why they have always found it difficult to live together, shifting from collaboration to outright rejection.

Taking this preliminary observation as our starting-point, my exploration of the connection between them will be divided into two parts.

In the first (and historically prior) stage I shall discuss the pre-eminence accorded to the female genitalia in the early, magical, phase of religion. There was a very distant and doubtless very long era when if not actually worshipped, they were at least treated with great respect, before certain religions began to integrate them into their understanding as the indispensable complement of the opposite sex. This was what I shall refer to as the era of *collaboration* between the female genitalia and the sacred.

In the second stage the female genitals were excluded, rejected, subjugated. What was the reason for this ostracism? How can it be explained, let alone justified? This is what might be called the era of *separation* and *exclusion*.

Of course this division and sequence are to a large extent artificial because attitudes towards the female sex have always been ambiguous, a mixture of denial and (albeit anxious) acknowledgment, but it does correspond in overall terms to a shift from one form of religion to another, from polytheism to monotheism, religions of many gods and goddesses to those affirming the sole transcendence of a divine Paternity.

Our journey through the inevitable chaos of the history of religions will be informed by analysis and interpretation of myths as well as so-called sacred texts.

Myths were for a long time regarded as fables, mere fictions to which no real credence could be attached, but today, following the work of philosophers such as Claude Lévi-Strauss and Paul Ricoeur, we see them as having a cognitive value. They tell us how humankind tried to understand the secret origins of the world and they also offer exemplary models of society. They cannot therefore be left out of our discussions of the female genitalia because they accord them a specific place in cosmogony and cosmology, as well as in the organisation of society and its relationship to the deity.

"Collaboration" between female genitalia and the sacred

This phase includes so-called "prehistoric" religions as well as the polytheistic religions of Greece and Rome, Ancient Egypt, the Celtic world and Africa.

In these religious spheres woman is omnipresent, symbolising that without which all life would vanish: fertility. She is represented in highly schematic form on the walls of caves as a downward-pointing triangle split by a vertical line, as well as in carvings of wood or bone. We find these Venuses with over-developed female characteristics—enormous breasts, huge belly and sometimes vulva open to the navel—from the Pyrenees to Lake Baikal. The head is barely indicated and in no sense personalised.

Were these paintings and sculptures objects of worship? Opinion is divided on that point but it does seem that woman was revered as the sole source of life. Male symbols and phalluses were rare because, we think, for a long time our ancestors did not understand the connection between the sexual act and pregnancy.

Life emerged from woman's genitals.

Can we say, then, that this was the triumphal era of the female sex? Undoubtedly yes, but perhaps not for woman as a human being because she was reduced to her function as the producer of life. Of course we must avoid any intellectual anachronism here, for it is likely that while there may have been no concept of woman as human being, neither was there one of man! Nevertheless, this does mark a first "reduction" of woman, the earliest female "functionalism" which would extend well beyond the "dawn of humanity" in which the survival of the species was the most important consideration.

The same thing is found in later and much more highly evolved civilisations such as that of Ancient Greece. Here woman was seen not as the sole source of life, but as a brood female. Gods and goddesses coupled in sacred marriages—hierogamies—which were often reproduced ritualistically at harvest time in a union between the king and the high priestess.

This was the era of the Mother Goddesses, whose names and attributes vary but who are, in the words of the historian of religions E. O. Jammes, "the most ancient manifestations of the concept of the deity."

51

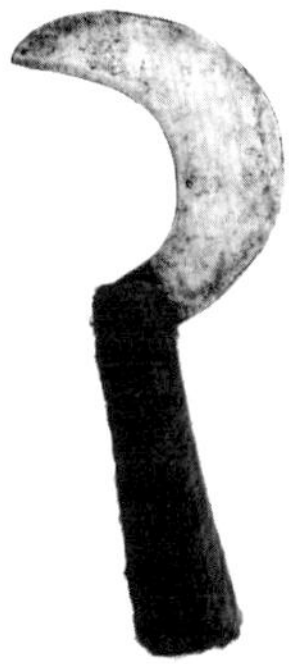

49

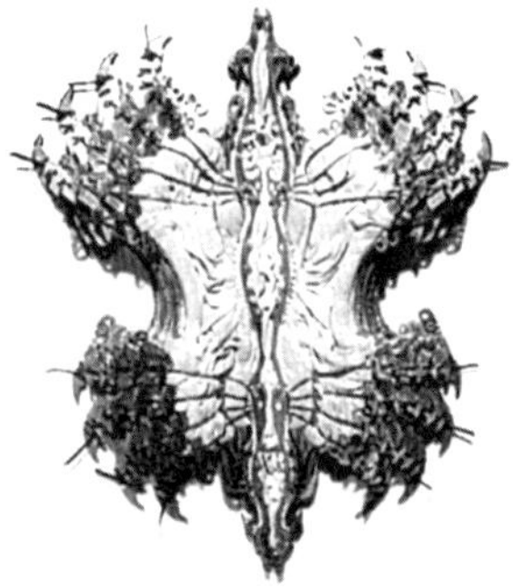

50

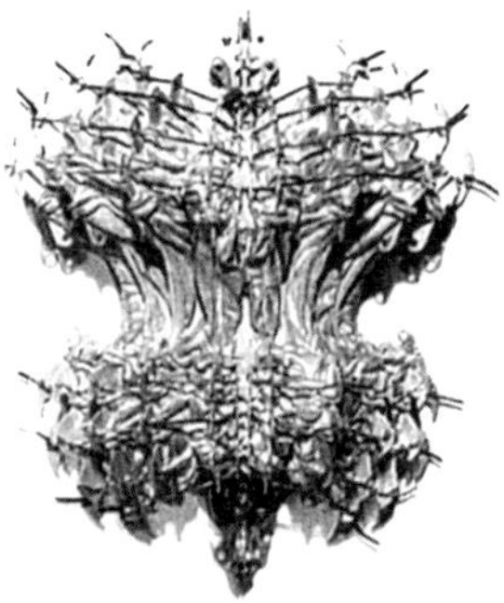

Some customs still maintain "therapeutics" destined to remove "evil" from the sexual organs, like excision and infibulation in which the female sexual organs no longer assume anything but the magisterial aspect of the "closed mouth".

Thus in a Sumerian hymn of the 3rd century BC the goddess Inina calls upon Dumuzzi, her brother or son or lover—the roles are confused because they are depersonalised, all that counts is the function of insemination—to come and fertilise her, in terms which confirm her status as Earth Mother: "Come plough my vulva".

Much later, an 11th-century engraving shows a woman barely emerging out of the earth to suckle two animals, an ox and a snake. She is a nature-goddess, nourishing the vegetable as well as the animal kingdom, as is shown by the plants that surround her.

In certain myths animals couple with women in order to pass on to them the strength of their species. Thus the Indians of the North-American plains thought that human society, whose survival was assured by the presence of many bison, had its origins in a transfer of vital energy between a bison and a woman, and they represented this copulation in their ritual dances.

In short, woman, from being the solitary producer of life, now became an instrument of it, an essential, privileged, even primordial one, but an instrument nonetheless. That change would weigh heavily on her position within societies and religions for a long time to come. Not that this female function is cause for regret, but simply that there was for a long time a temptation to limit woman to it and only consider her being on that basis. But, as Sylviane Agacinski puts it, "Motherhood... is a model of creation which is not incompatible with all other forms of creativity and expression."[1]

It should be added (a point less often stressed) that in what might be regarded as certain more highly evolved religions, women were also seen as instruments of spirituality. In the Taoist religion of China, for instance, or in Indian Tantric religious practices, sex can be a vehicle for achieving ecstasy in the etymological sense of the word, i.e. standing outside the self (ex-stare). Sexual union can lead a man to a state of mind and body which helps bring about not exactly a fusion with the divine (because

[1] Sylviane Agacinski, *Politique des sexes*, collection Points. Editions du Seuil, Paris, 2001, p.99.

these religions do not have an all-powerful creative Deity), but a sort of personal transcendence. By holding back his sperm the man strengthens his own spiritual essence.

On this point, an ancient Chinese text tells how a mythical emperor, Houang-ti, rose straight to heaven because in the course of his life he had coupled with one thousand two hundred women, having been initiated into the arts of love by three of them.

Here again we see man using woman as an intermediary to preserve his vital powers by nourishing, through non-ejaculation and refusing to spill his seed, what might be regarded as the essence of masculinity. The woman's pleasure, so delicately cultivated, is used in the service of the man's metamorphosis and the sexual act is, once more, ritualised.

Everyone knows of the famous Kama Sutra, written between the 3rd and the 5th centuries by an Indian sage who describes all the techniques that can lead to ecstasy. People in the West generally misread it as a treatise on eroticism. In fact, the Kama Sutra presents the sex act as a sacred ritual whose goal is not just physical but spiritual, primarily for the man.

Thus, even where Eastern religions did take women's own sexuality into account, they did so not for the sake of women themselves and in the context of a genuine human relationship, but with regard to the male seeking to transcend his human limitations and experience an alternative mental state. Remember that for Hindus the cosmos was engendered by the sexual sport of the god Shiva with his paredra the goddess Sakti. Her role here is certainly important—without her vital energy the world would probably never have been made manifest—but she is an aid, nothing more. This, in very schematic terms, is how what I have called the collaboration between the sacred and the female genitals works in practice. Woman is the producer of life, a brood female, life's instrument and even, for man, an instrument of the life of the mind, of spirituality. For this reason she is frequently deified. She is a mother-goddess, or a goddess taking part, with a male god, in the creation of life.

Did this (partial) enhancement of woman's status have any influence on her standing within societies and belief systems?

As far as the prehistoric period is concerned, we can do no more than present tentative hypotheses. We can only surmise that the earliest men and women lived in a state of promiscuity and equality between the sexes, until such time as men, having realised their role in procreation, started to appropriate women in order to ensure their own personal descendance. What role did women play in religion? We have no idea.

In the still ancient but better-known societies of the Egyptians, Aztecs, Celts and others in which polytheism was practised, women did participate in religious life. Thus in Egyptian religion they could exercise a sacred function and some goddesses had their own priestesses; but more often, women in the temples played secondary roles as singers, dancers or servants to the god. Likewise, in the Aztec religions girls would commit themselves to celibacy and the priesthood. As priestesses they looked after the temple, offering up incense and playing a key role in ceremonies.

In short, woman could sometimes play an important part in religious observance, i.e. in society's concrete relationship to the deity, and her sexuality could even enter directly into the sphere of the sacred. For these female servants of the god or goddess were often required to observe celibacy—as with the Roman vestals—or, on the contrary, take part in ritual prostitution, like the holy prostitutes. Herodotus relates that every Babylonian woman had to go to the temple once in her life and copulate for a fixed price with any stranger. The money she made in this way would be offered to the goddess in witness to her initiation into the cult of the sex deity. The female genitals were thus omnipresent and all-powerful in the realm of the gods...

Exclusion relationship between female genitalia and the sacred

Then came the monotheistic religions of Judaism, Christianity and Islam, with their male God the Father: sole paternity by a God with complete power over the creation and government of the world.

*"The vagina which leads to the womb,
it's there that
evil starts"
(cf. Leqeu, caption for illustration 52)*

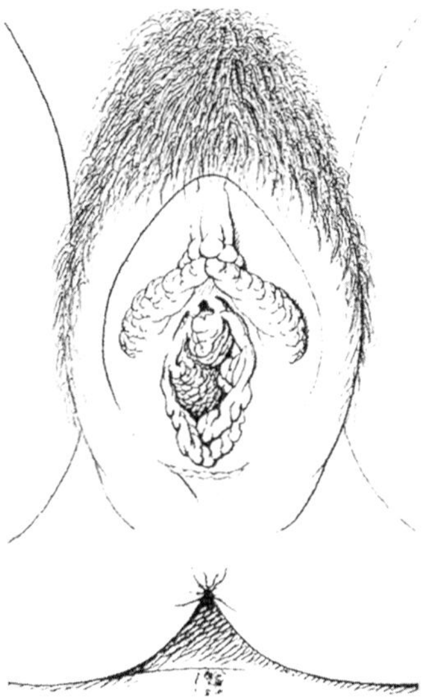

52

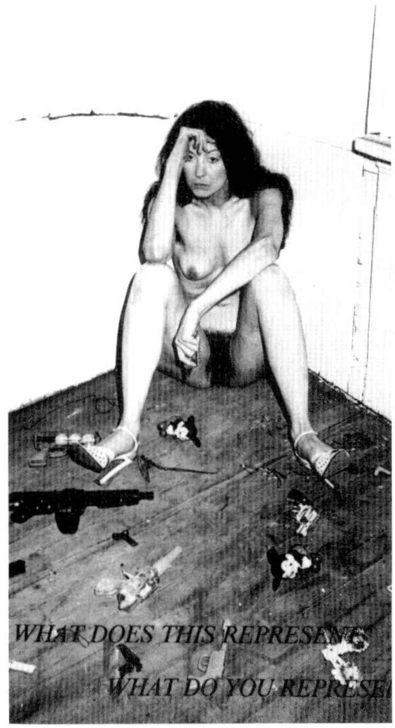

53

What then happens to the female aspect? It is relegated to a secondary position in rituals and excluded from the institutions, teaching and message of theology. Woman rabbis are rare in Judaism. The Catholic church has no women priests and Islam separates women from men in religious observance and teaching.

Why should this be?

Is this exclusion rooted in the holy books of those religions, the Bible and the Koran? In fact it is based on a interpretation of them, an interpretation always made by men.

Take, for instance, the Bible, and in particular the Book of Genesis, which as we know presents two successive versions of the creation of man and woman. In Genesis 1, 27 we read: "So God created man in his own image; in the image of God he created him; male and female he created them". In Genesis 2, written at a different time, God gives Adam a companion called Eve, formed from one of his ribs. Eve is his "helpmate and partner".

How did the male exegetes interpret this double story? They neglected the first version which does not imply the superiority of man over woman, since man as the image of the deity is both male and female, and deduced from the second that Eve, who was made from Adam, is an inferior being. Moreover it is she who leads Adam into disobedience. She thus bears responsibility for sin. In Ecclesiasticus (Sirach) 25, 24 it is written: "Of the woman came the beginning of sin, and through her we all die". So for millennia woman would carry a curse and be burdened with guilt! Certain feminist women theologians, on the other hand, believe and write, as we are reminded by Elisabeth Parmentier, that by taking humankind out of the Garden of Eden, Eve allowed us to discover "the joy of learning, the delights of beauty and knowledge." Without Eve, quips one German woman theologian, "we would still be up in the trees".[2]

One sura in the Koran states unequivocally that "men have authority over women by virtue of the preference shown to them by God" (Koran 3, 34).

[2] *La Femme, ce qu'en disent les religions*, Editions de l'Atelier, Paris, 2002.

As for the Buddha, he wrote nothing but did initially oppose the idea that women, in order to attain Enlightenment, could practise renunciation (bhikkuni) in the same way as men, and his foster mother had to insist before the first female community could be founded. Even then it remained subject to the authority of male monks and was governed by stricter rules than its male counterparts. Women were so weak it was impossible to over-supervise their activities!

Thus in these religions woman is considered not only as an inferior but also as a dangerous, even evil being who must be subjugated to man's authority, excluded from religious structures and institutions and banned from using the language of theology.

Yet her ontological equality is also proclaimed by these same religions.

In Christianity, for instance, St Paul declares that after Christ, "there is no such thing as Jew and Greek, slave and freeman, male and female" (Galatians 3, 28). Christ himself had not hesitated to surround himself with women. Some of the apostles may have been women, although they are never quoted. All four Evangelists refer to the presence of Mary Magdalene, the sinner of Galilee, though her words are rarely reported. Jesus opposes the stoning of the adulteress, she who has sinned through her sex (John 8, 3), cures the woman suffering from haemorrhages (Matthew 9, 22) , which society of the time considered impure, and, on Easter morning, addresses a group of women to entrust them with the immense task of reporting Christianity's most fundamental moment, the Resurrection.

Judaism also affirms the original equality of men and women.

In Islam, a sura proclaims this same equality with respect to the deity and the life to come.

So how can we explain the fact that in these three religions and others women have been kept in a state of subordination and excluded in particular from that central aspect of all religious observance, sacrifice? Why are they forbidden from being, in the words of Georges Dumezil, "bearers of the sacred"?

The first point to make is that "profane" philosophy had already prepared the ground for this devaluation of woman. Did Aristotle not write, as early as the 4th century BC, that "in all species the male always prevails over the female. The human race is no exception"? In other words, man is superior by nature to woman. This probably indicates a biological misapprehension of what it is to be female, but later scientific progress in the field brought about little change in the opinions of those thinkers who followed. Schopenhauer would deny women the right to hold property because, as beings who were but "intermediary between children and men", they were incapable of so doing. "It would be better", he added, "and in the interests of women themselves, for polygamy to be reintroduced and so return them to their normal status of beings destined by nature to obey." Lacking reason and the power of logical thought, they had to rely on lies and trickery. Nietzsche, for his part, even questioned woman's ability to think about her own condition. "Let it suffice for her", he said, "to exercise the arts in which she has such skill, those of pleasing, of taking away their men's cares, soothing their pain, and accepting with delicate docility the amiable (male) desires which are directed towards her." Worried by the few attempts at liberation of his day, he even declared: "The emancipation of women is one of the most remarkable symptoms of the decline in those instincts most essentially feminine"... Many more philosophical quotations from various periods could be given but that would serve no purpose, for it is already clear that society in its intellectual, civil and political spheres practised the systematic denigration of women. The religions might, indeed should have remained true to their fundamental ideals and vocations, by proclaiming the equality of all. They did not do so. They fell into line with society, adopting its prejudices and sometimes anticipating and inducing them. This would be a very serious matter for their future.

At the same time, it seems that men, having seized power in the religious institutions, excluded women from them because they were afraid of the attraction they could exert. Convincing evidence for this can be seen, once again in a Christian context, in the advice given by St Paul and the Fathers of the Church, the first theologians: "Let women", writes Tertullian in the 2nd century, "renounce all finery and conceal even their

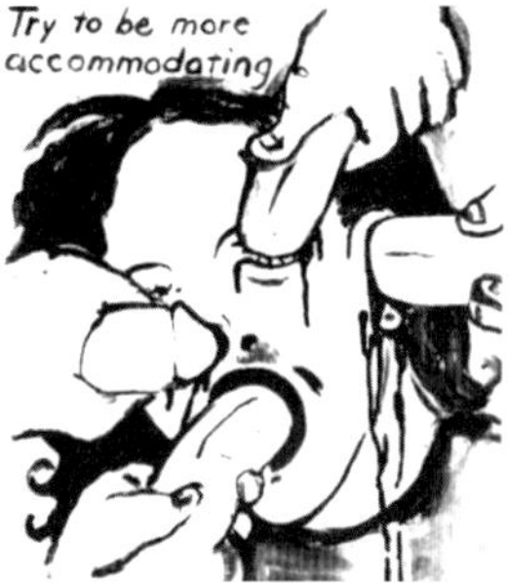

55

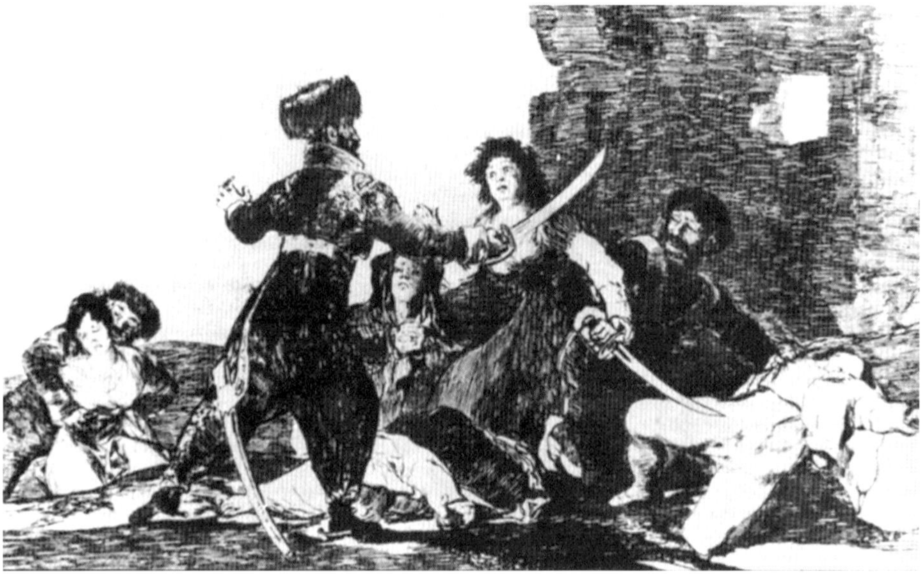

54

...no longer let oneself be violated

natural charm so as not to be objects of temptation for men". Women were thus considered to be an opportunity for sin, sin being for centuries assimilated to the sexual act that Adam and Eve were said to have performed. So no more women, no more temptation, and no more sin! The female sex was excluded because it was likely to be prejudicial to spirituality, if only through the desire it awakened, a desire that let the body gain ascendancy over the mind.

Moreover the female being, marked by the blood of menstruation and the blood of childbirth, was regarded as impure. In Judaism all contact with a woman is forbidden during her period and she is required to purify herself afterwards by ritual bathing. Certain Muslims in the Caucasus, on the other hand, shut their women away in specially-built huts while they are menstruating. Christianity does not make a link between loss of blood and impurity but old Orthodox traditions prevent menstruating women from taking communion. There is an incompatibility between female sexuality, marked by blood, and the sacred. It seems generally true therefore that women's faculty of periodically losing blood and of giving life in the bloody process of childbirth fills men with real horror. For centuries it must have generated in them an anxious perplexity mixed with fear, or envy of that prodigious power of life-giving which is the privilege of women.

It still remained to be said, and it was said, that women could not play an important part in religious life because they were too physically and intellectually weak to take on important tasks. It was said and repeated, provoking in the Christian sphere the indignation of certain contemporary female theologians. There is no way, they say, that physical weakness can be a barrier to participation in worship or administration of the institutions; as for intellectual weakness, that was perpetuated for a long time by the ignorance in which women were kept of their religion. A weakness that was claimed to be theirs by nature made it possible, in religions as in society, to subjugate women.

And that seemed all the more necessary as it was impossible to trust a sex so characterised by ambiguity, itself also natural. Woman is at once angel and demon. St John of Chrysostome described her in these terms at the start of the 4th century: "Woman is ... ineluctable grief, natural temptation, desirable calamity, delectable scourge, natural evil brightly painted". She is therefore evil, "calamity", "scourge", but she is also "ineluctable", "desirable", "delectable". She cannot be cast out because that would be a sin but neither can she be trusted—this is a dangerous sex!—so she must be restricted to working in subordinate roles. The only things about her that are praiseworthy are those declared to be positive for men: obedience, gentleness, mercy, compassion, devotion, etc.

The opposition is one between the Virgin Mary and Eve, or the much-discussed Lilith, created before Eve. This Lilith, who is mentioned by the Prophet Isaiah, had left Adam, her equal, because she refused to accept that he had power over her. After that she is said to have become very friendly with Samael, angel of darkness, and never returned to the Garden of Eden. She was a formidable seductress who very quickly sank into oblivion; but she was also perhaps the first woman to evade the power of man and God, at least if we believe all the interpretations that have been put forward of this little-known character.

In truth it is not really the genitalia of woman that are rejected by patriarchal religions after having been revered in others, it is the female being in its whole physical, moral and intellectual extension. Of woman's moral and intellectual specificities, man has only kept and, over the centuries and within religions, given value to those which both corresponded to his desire for power, and could assuage the fear that the opposite sex inspired in him.

Emergence of a female being?

How can religions put an end to this process of forgetting and concealment against which women today are protesting? It is a huge task. They must first find the courage to return to the founding texts which generally posit equality between men and women with respect to the deity; return to the founding texts and offer a reading of them which is not exclusively masculine, but masculine and feminine at the same time. The same goes for the myths.

Then they must look again at certain apocryphal and Gnostic texts such as the Gospel of Miriam de Madgala (also known as Mary Magdalene), which is part of what is called the "Berlin Codex". In them they would find "the whole feminine dimension of early Christianity" which has clearly been subsequently repressed.

Finally, they should lend their support to a new anthropology and a new theology.

This anthropology would recognise, in common with the psychologist of the depths of the mind, Carl Gustav Jung, that there is in each being, whether man or woman, a feminine part, the *anima*, and a masculine part, the *animus*, which can join together in a quest for the divine.

Religions might even emphasise that in order to increase the scope of spirituality, it is necessary to turn to the anima. That is what St John of the Cross is doing when he, a man, experiences what it is like to be the Bride of whom the Song of Songs speaks. That is what, in a quite different context, the shamans of Siberia are doing when, in ceremonies intended to bring them into contact with the deity, they feminise their voices, clothes and behaviour. Spirituality draws heavily on the feminine side of human beings, so it comes as no surprise that a 14th-century Rhenish theologian, Master Eckhart, should have written: "Woman, the most noble word that could be addressed to the soul". Nor is it any surprise that the majority of mystics have been women, including St Theresa of Avila and Hildegard of Bingen, who described their union with the deity in such passionate terms that people wondered whether their experience was also sexual. In fact, in the deepest mystical experience sex, and particularly the female sex, has its place. There is a connection between erotic activity and the spiritual.

Thus, to neglect or devalue the feminine part in every human being, as religions have done, is to deprive spirituality of one of its privileged

56

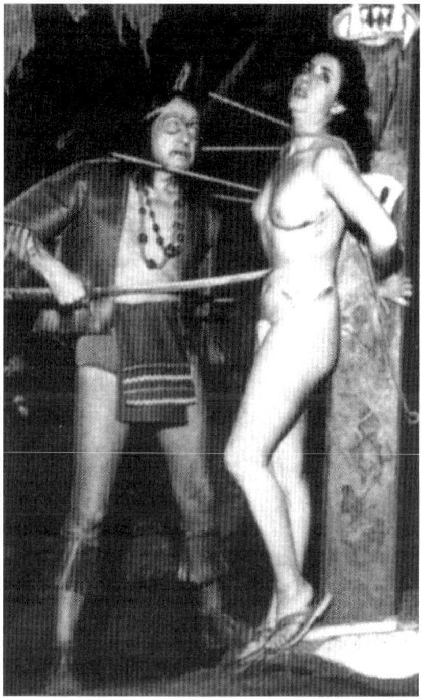

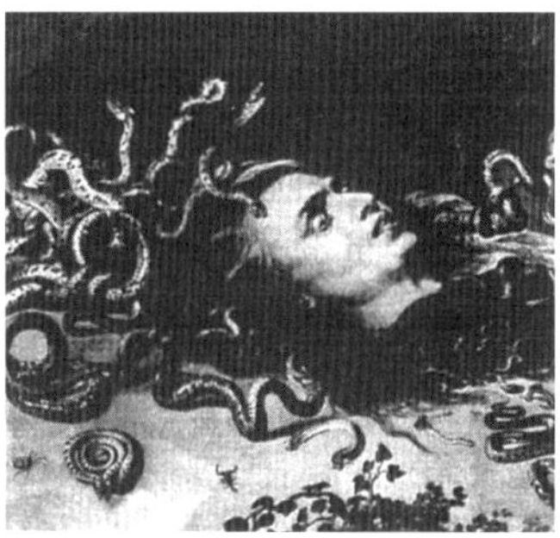

57

58

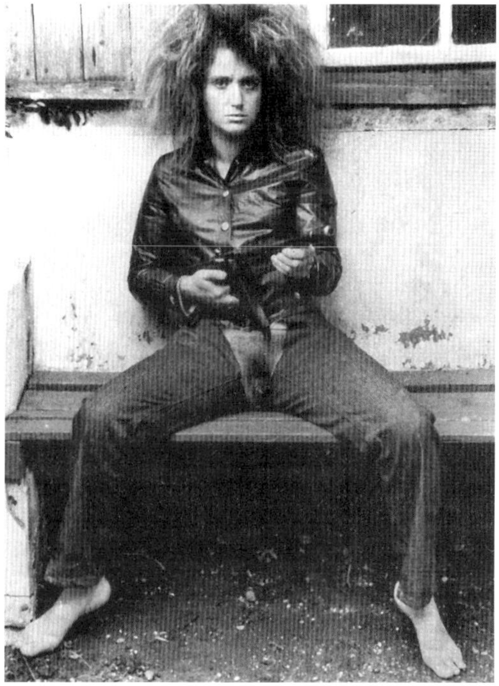

… …no longer let oneself be assaulted

modes of access to the divine. Restoring it to its rightful place and role would rehabilitate the feminine, and woman, in the religious sphere.

As for the deity itself, it is interesting to note that it has often been understood and represented as bisexual. A bearded Aphrodite was found in Cyprus and a bald Venus in Italy. The Greek god Dionysus used to dress as a woman, Zervan, the Iranian god, was androgynous, as was the supreme Chinese deity of darkness and light, while the Indian god Vishnu manifests himself in "avatars" that are sometimes men and sometimes women! There is thus a tradition of divine bisexuality.

Does this mean that religions of the Father are the only ones not to have recognised this complementarity requiring the feminine to be placed on the same footing as the masculine? No, for several Judaic Midrashim present Adam as having been androgynous, or a man on his right side and a woman on his left. According to Scot Erigenes, a philosopher and Christian theologian of the 9th century, sexual division is a consequence of sin. That is when it began, and it will end, some time in the future, with the reunification of humankind. Christ for his part has already unified the sexes in his own nature, for after his resurrection he is neither male nor female. Unfortunately, in the monotheistic religions of Judaism, Christianity and Islam all this is rarely mentioned.

There nevertheless remains the recurrent fact that even in religions of the Father, the perfection of being, the being of primordial humans and of the deity, consists in a Unity and Totality in which sexual differences are erased. To the extent that, according to Jung, Christianity's holy Trinity lacks the feminine element necessary for its completeness. That is why in his view Mary, the mother of the son of God and a woman, should be added to the masculine Trinity. Which is incidentally what the recent dogma of the Assumption (1950), according to which the feminine managed to join with divine masculine, has belatedly suggested. In Christianity there has been, in the words of Yse Tardan-Masquelier, "a resistance to the complete recognition of the feminine principle", so that it was only in the 20th century that the masculine holy Trinity was expanded into a "quaternity" to include the feminine.

When the scale of the task of putting an end to a scandalous inequality in religions is presented in this way, it shows that what is required is not just a change of religious expression and practice, but a complete transformation of religions themselves, which will no doubt be an enrichment whose full implications cannot yet be measured.

For women, if religion is regarded as making demands upon the totality of a person (mind, feelings, sexuality ...), this will also be a crucial moment in the emergence of a feminine being which the shift from collaboration to exclusion in the relationship between sex and the sacred has yet to bring about. For if sex is made sacred, as in prehistoric religions and certain polytheistic ones, then woman is limited to an organ and its function; whereas if it is demonised, as in the patriarchal religions, she is amputated of that part of herself on which her specificity depends.

Where then is woman's being? It remains an unknown, not least to herself. It has been, by masculine discourse operating in all domains—religion, philosophy, politics, literature ...—stolen from her.

59

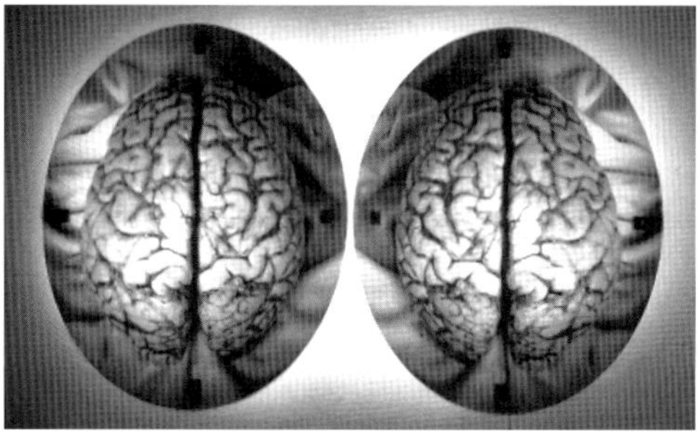

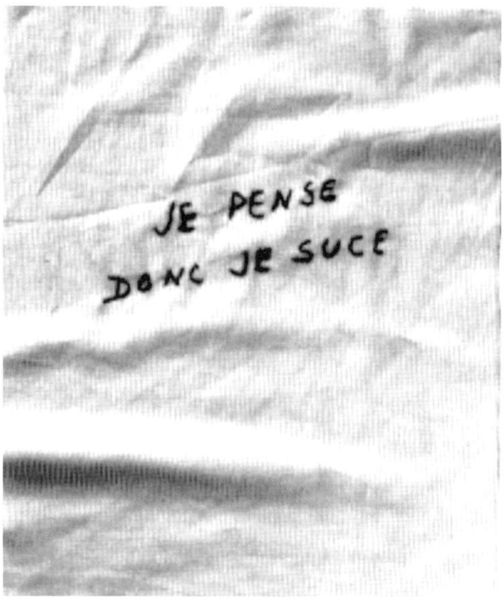

60

… laugh at misogyny
and the degradation it spreads.

Virgin or Demonness
Woman in Fin-de-Siècle Fantasies

Throughout the ages, the representation of the female genitals and of feminine sexuality presents a set of constants that manifest the sedimentation in the collective imaginary of all the distorted narratives relating the originary abjection of woman and the horror and disgust inspired by the black hole of her sex. Why then should one take a more specific interest in the mystifications of the nineteenth century, and specifically its latter half, rather than probing all the way to the depths of this sedimentary layer? There are several reasons. The first is that the nineteenth century, which we think of as long behind us, is the origin point of the fantasies that would be conveyed by modernity. To be sure, the roots of these fantasies plunge further back in time. They are part and parcel of the double Judeo-Christian and Hellenic basis of our Western culture. But by combing through the myths and legends to nourish its hatred of the feminine, the nineteenth century reactivated these primal fantasies and put them into circulation again. And with this reactivation, it tore them free from their archaic context and set them up solidly within the modern imaginary. Freud's famous text on the female sex, paralyzing and hideous like Medusa's head, is but one example. This reinstallation of the old fantasies, which found its best ally in the scientific and medical discourses of the time, long informed artistic, literary and more broadly social representations. The figures of hysteria which were then portrayed are fortunately no longer with us. Yet it is nonetheless uncertain whether we are totally unburdened of these tenacious prejudices that haunted the nineteenth century. As proof, I would point to certain works by female artists or writers who claim or believe to be liberated by exposing their sexual fantasies, and whose purely reactive gesture shows on the contrary the extent to which they remain confined to a provocative acceptance, tributary to the stereotypes, the clichés and the commonplaces with which male speech has cloaked the feminine, and which the nineteenth century brought to a delirious paroxysm.

The second justification for this choice of a faraway and yet paradoxically proximate age (if only via psychoanalysis, invented at the time) is that the figure of woman is omnipresent in the nineteenth century. She is in painting, she is in literature, she is in decorative art; but also, in an obsessive way, she is in medical tomes, essays of scientific psychology, treatises of moral philosophy. Never has an epoch known such an obsession with the feminine. Rather than an obsession, it would be preferable to speak of a "nightmare of the feminine." For what we find is a Sabbath's dance of diabolical figures, Salome, Herodias, Judith, Delila, Messalina, Medea, not to speak of Omphale, Cleopatra, the Queen of Sheba or Helen of Troy, all of whom use their malevolent powers of seduction to destroy men. The myths, the legends, the religious history, furnish figures in which the fantasmatic fear of the feminine can be embodied. For if the feminine is omnipresent, it is beneath the form of a sex that fascinates and arouses fear, attracts and repels, disquiets, disturbs, troubles. Everywhere are statements of the danger that men risk before the silent appeal of her mouth of shadows. The fantasy mingles with the very real fear of syphilis. Des Esseintes, the Huysmans character to whom Mallarmé devoted a piece of verse, sees purulent syphilis in a dream, seeking like a ghoul to press her crackled lips and poisoned sex against his own. For she is the Glutonness: the devouring woman of the fatal embrace.

Let us note that even though this century explores the full, accursed range of legendary female figures, it speaks of woman as though of a species in her own right: a unique species, having nothing to do with men, who are psychologically different and to whom the singular would not apply.[1] This generic conception of woman comes from the idea, commonly held by scientists and men of letters at the time, that behind all the cultural appearances that mask the call of the womb, women are moved by their instinct of generation alone. For example, the great criminologist of the time, Lambroso, insists on the fact that that men are original, whereas women are typical. By that, he does not simply mean that women are related to the "eternal feminine" exploited by literature across the ages, but that woman constitutes a species in the zoological sense of the term.

Woman Is All Sex

From the above it follows that women can be treated as naturalists treat animal species, and men hardly hesitated to do so! But in reality, such a treatment amounts to denying women a part of their humanity. Which was no doubt the hidden intention.

This does not mean that all the clichés, all the stereotypes about women that have crisscrossed our history from the most ancient texts of Greco-Roman mythology and from Biblical narratives were simply cast aside in favor of this naturalistic vision. On the contrary, they were taken up anew, magnified, tirelessly restaged. Women are deceitful. Women are untrustworthy. Women are wrongdoers. From Eve to Pandora, the female sex has only generated misfortune. The fabliaux of the Middle Ages, the tales, the comedies, all exploit the humorous aspect of these problems. The same themes appear more disquieting in the nineteenth century, because they are portrayed as the operation of the genitals

[1] On this theme, as on the Lilith myth, one should read the excellent book by Mireille Dottin Orsini: *Cette femme quíon dit fatale*. It was in this essay, whose intuitions meet my own in many cases, that I found the quote from Flaubert and the reference to the ancient belief in the little animal hiding in the depths of the vagina. One can also usefully consult: *Idols of Perversity: Fantasies of feminine evil in fin de siècle culture*, by Bram Djikstra; *Femmes fin de siècle*, by Michèle Friang; *Les Filles de Noces – Misère sexuelle et prostitution* au XIXe siècle by Alain Corbin.

themselves. And the female sex is disturbing. In Ancient Greece, Baubo got people to laugh by showing the crack in her underbelly and her great, gaping lips. Courbet's painting, L'Origine du Monde, arouses fascination mingled with a fear that seeks to hide beneath the mask of excited interest. The painting, which speaks so loudly of the fears of the time, actually says this: woman is all sex. Not only because she uses her sex to seduce—that is, strictly speaking, to turn man aside from his straight and narrow path, like Omphale having Hercules lie down at her feet or Cleopatra holding Anthony in her power—but also because she is perpetually in heat. This was Baudelaire's phrase. Her sex that opens up to nocturnal depths is insatiable, constantly asking for more. Hypersexualization is always one of the symptoms whereby an anxiety-creating vision of the other is conveyed. We know the colonial stereotype of the super-potent black man and the indigenous woman with her animal aroticism. In the nineteenth century, woman is a figure of this "other" in whom an ill-tamed nature can reawaken. The witch, in the Middle Ages, straddles her broom to go to the infernal Sabbath; and we can easily see the erotic meaning of this masturbatory straddling. Of course a woman is always, more or less, a witch in search of a broomstick to rub her sex on. Far from destroying these archaic images, medical discourse would lend them the weight of its clinical authority. Painting and literature could then take them up unabashedly.

What, indeed, does Courbet paint, under a title with cosmological connotations: The Origin of the World? Not the Great Mother, with the generous oversexualization of a pagan idol, whence all the world's creatures spring, nor the Good Goddess with her fertile womb, but a desymbolized female sex: the female sex in its physiological nudity; the female sex without what tames it in our culture, woman in her lovable form with her angelic face, her rounded shoulders, her soft arms, her delicate hands, her fine ankles. Doesn't this cruel framing, which deprives the feminine of its cultural allure, make Courbet into the most faithful, most realistic portraitist of this species which, in the masculine imaginary, is indistinguishable from its sex?

Lilith, or Woman in Heat

This confusion, which makes it possible to deny women any but a sexual identity, finds a new fantasmatic legitimacy in the myth of Lilith, as Rémy de Gourmont rewrote it for the theater. Lilith is the fallen female being who precedes Eve and about which the Bible story, as commonly taught, is almost silent. Of all the resurrections, the one proposed by Rémy de Gourmont touches closest upon misogynist fantasy. In this sense it is exemplary. To believe him, Lilith is a creature who, like Adam later on, was made of clay. But because God was short of material to finish sculpting her, He took away a handful of clay from her belly, so as to give her a head. The anecdote is rich with meaning. It tells us first of all that Lilith, the accursed ancestor of all women, and prototype of the generic Woman, has no brain, or or rather, instead of a brain she has a sex, since it is her underbelly that has been used to create the organ of intelligence whereby man is distinguished from the animal. Next it tells us that she has a hole in place of her sex, which is no less terrifying, as Freud would later show. Finally it tells us that in woman, high and low are inversed, which alone is enough to render her diabolical. We then understand why the struggle of masculine against feminine takes, to quote Flaubert, the form of "the brain's protest against the womb."

"Woman is abominable because she is natural." The phrase is Baudelaire's. It is well known and often quoted. But those who quote it generally forget to mention what follows, which completes the remark and in a sense explains it. They are wrong to forget, because the meaning of the accusation of naturality directed against women can only be understood in reference to the scornful observation that the poet makes of the woman's sexual avidity: "She is always in heat and wants to be fucked." Perhaps without knowing it, Baudelaire states in these crude and cruel words the veritable reason of the disgust that woman arouses in civilized man. Through the insatiable sex that commands her, woman has remained at a level of almost animal nature. What is therefore so disturbing in this detestable creature is the constant recall to nature's order that is sounded by her sex, and that pulls man backwards, toward the nether depths of his animal origins. Let us then understand that what makes women so abominable is ultimately the fact that she speaks the truth of origins. Courbet made no mistake. His painting is not about the origin of children, i.e. the birth of each individual, but about the origin of humanity, or the animal prehistory of man.

The Animal Nature of the Female Sex

We have a hard time measuring the effects of evolutionism today. They run deep. Man suddenly became conscious of the fact that he had not been created alone, in the image of God as he was told by the Bible; instead he partook of the animal kingdom. How then to define the man's humanity, if not by a severance from this origin, and therefore by an overvaluation of the reign of culture to the detriment of nature? But woman, who since the origin of time had been considered close to nature, represents the greatest obstacle to this labor of nature's eradication. For in her, everything is nature. Beginning with her genitals, which are devoted to this natural task: procreation, i.e. the propagation of the species. Woman is therefore the being whereby nature makes itself remembered within humanity. She is consequently an object of hatred. Her sex, whereby man pays his tribute to nature, draws humanity down toward its origin, now become abject in his eyes since it was discovered to be animal. The fantasies engendered at the time by sexuation and by feminine sexuality were reactivated by Darwinism.

An old belief held that in the woman's uterus, where man's gaze could not penetrate, a sort of untamed animal was hidden. The nineteenth century no longer believed in this tomfoolery, even if there remains a kind of trace or remanence in the form of the fantasy of the vagina dentata. For this century, everything about the female sex evokes bestiality. Let's take the case of the young boy who, in Freud's text on the

61

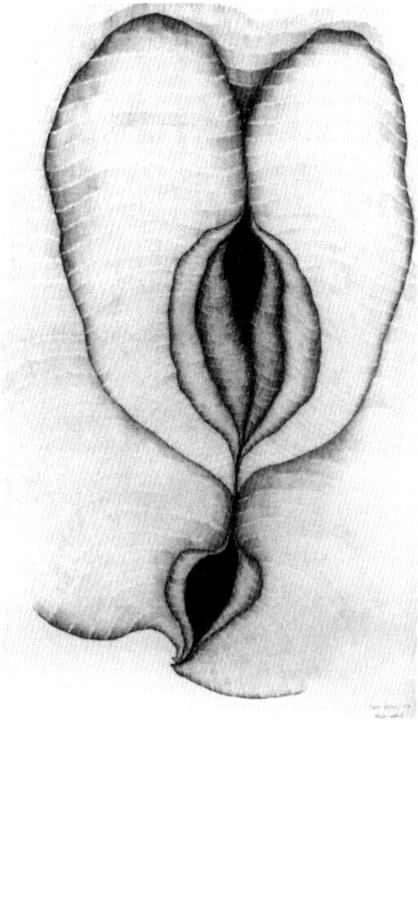

62

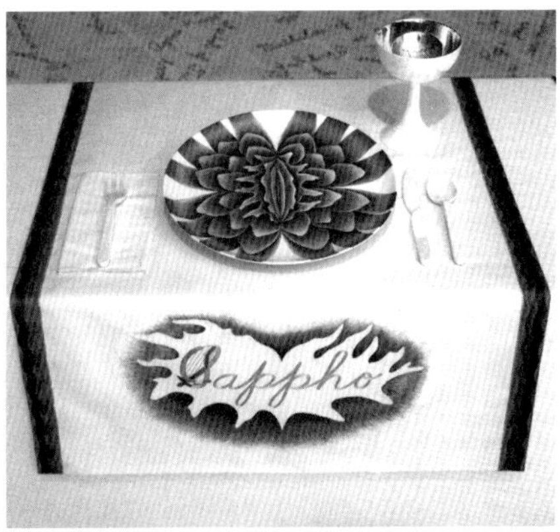

…and sanctify the female sexual organs

Medusa's head, discovers his mother's sex, which is actually nothing, and whose absence at her hairy lower belly evokes the Medusa's head. Medusa is a Gorgon sister who was proud of her hair, until it was transformed into hideous serpents. The child sees these threatening serpents which curl around the mouth of the vagina. Beneath this animal proliferation he no longer recognizes his mother. And he remains petrified with fright. Medusa, as the myth also tells us, is she who petrifies all those who look upon her. Such is the woman's sex for Freud. The fear it arouses comes from its emptiness, but also from the hairs that mask and underline it at the same time. In the academic painting that portrays, not woman, but the ideal figures that take her place, the sex of the nudes is hairless like those of statues, and dead like their eyes. Courbet is a realist artist. He paints what is, or at least what he thinks he sees. And what he sees is abundant hair, also called "fourrure" (fur) or "toison" (fleece). Manet is also a realist painter; he cannot lie about the hairy truth of the genitals, thus Olympia negilently lays her hand over the pussy that we must not see, and whose bestiality is embodied by the little black cat that glides through the painting. There is another figuration of the same fantasy. This time we owe it to an academic painter, JérÙme, and the canvas is entitled Le combat des coqs (The Cockfight). In an Arcadian landscape, a young man and a young woman lie beside each other. They have the androgynous beauty that desexualizes human beings; it is pictorially accentuated by the way their modeled flesh is covered in glossy varnish. They watch two cocks fighting in the foreground of the scene. The brushtrokes are violent. The colors are loud. Feathers fly in all directions. Visibly what is not happening between the two ethereal creatures is taking place in the confrontation of these two beasts given over to their instincts, as though to say that sexuality always has to do with the animal nature of humanity. And woman, by her supposed proximity to nature, serves within representation as the imaginary agent of this dehumanization. She is therefore not only "abominable" but also dangerous.

Philosophy always springs from the imaginary. If Schopenhauer is rediscovered with passion at the century's close, it is because in his misogyny, the philosopher held that woman was no more than an instrument whose pleasant exterior was used by nature to trap man in order to make him serve its own ends, which are none other than self-perpetuation. In her games of seduction, says the philosopher, woman's sole aim is to lead man toward her sex, so as to ensure the continuation of the species. Hence the horror inspired in man by this fecund hole whose avidity obeys a pure call of nature, and not a desire mastered by culture. Human animality is what speaks through this ventriloquist organ, and this is the voice that must be silenced at all costs. Hide that sex... By opposition, the ideal woman is the virgin whose sex is still mute, or even better, she is an android devoid of sexuality, whose sex will never speak. In other words, the nightmare is the "natural" woman, while the dream is the creature born of Edison's art, and not the fruit of sexuated reproduction: the future Eve.[2] Does she have between her legs that orifice that the Middle Ages called the devil's door? The novel remains discreet on the subject, but whatever the case, any embrace with this artificial doll is doomed to sterility. Liberated from her procreative function, the woman rediscovers the romantic charm that makes her an angel. The angels don't have any sex, it's well known, and above all not that hole that opens up to hell, the hell that in the nineteenth century takes on the face of originary animality. Twice virgin Mary, virgin of all penetration and virgin of original sin, becomes an ideal figure to be worshipped. The dogma of the Immaculate Conception is of this age. And the male begins to dream: Oh, if woman could be a Mary conceived outside the original sin of animality that weighs down humanity... If she could conceive a being who would thereby be exonerated from all that...

Seductive Nature

The future Eve, who escapes the laws of nature inscribed deeply in

[2] Title of the novel by Villiers de lÍlsle-Adam.

63

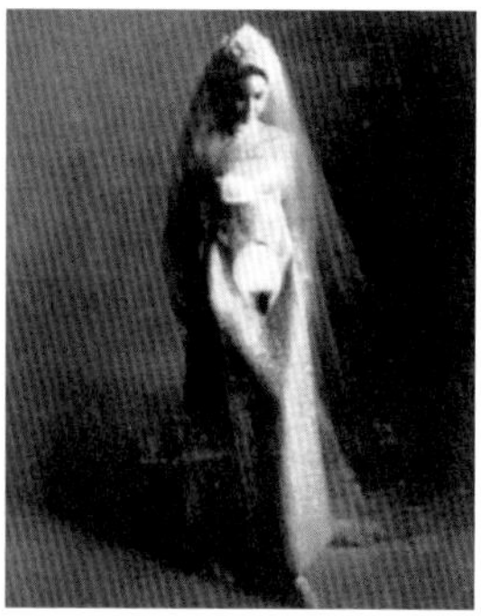

64

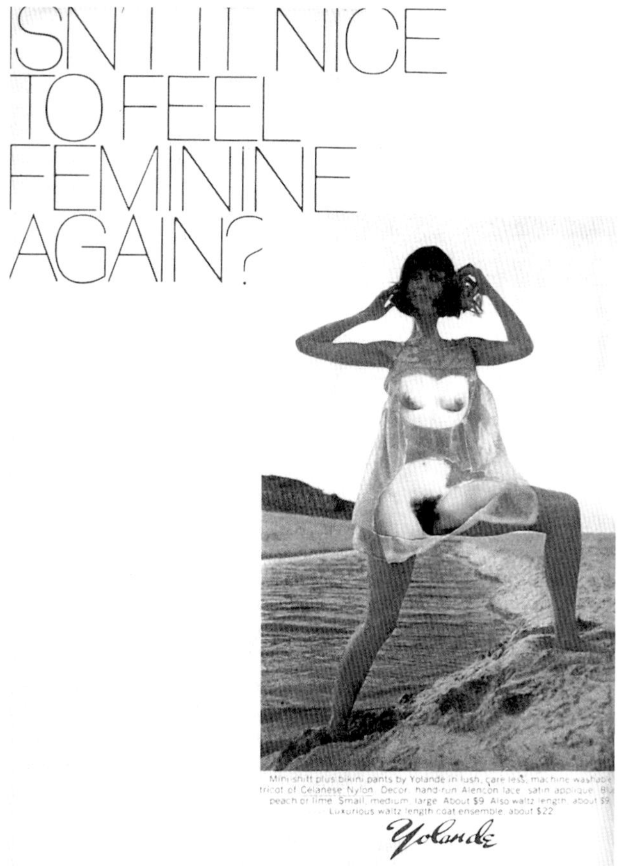

...to release it from its yokes

the gaping female sex, reconciles the century with the feminine, if only for a moment of fiction. As though this dissociation between woman and nature, between sexuality and procreation, were necessary for woman to become once again the charming (and not diabolically charmed) face of humanity. This observation leads one to wonder whether the current perspectives of the desexualization of reproduction by cloning are not deep representations of a sex that terrified the imagination.

In the nineteenth century, women who use their nature to reach their natural ends are considered frightening. Eternally childlike, perverse women—Salome of course, but also Nana, Carmen, Lulu, who set men aflame and cause them to lose their heads. Redoubtable, these seductresses who play on their beguiling sex without even knowing what they are doing, because what was long attributed to feminine ruse is now conceived as a ruse of nature. If woman had a strategic intelligence, man could outwit its tricks; but there are none. As in the animal kingdom, instinct alone guides the female. Woman is therefore all the deadlier in that her sex is a pure instrument, on which nature can strike chords that drive the wisest man to madness.

Having no cultural appropriation of herself, woman represents a threat for the order that culture has established. Consequence: she is a social danger. She is Nana, obscene on the stage that displays her in her flesh-colored tights. She is Nana, the golden gadfly, who puts Paris in heat and sows trouble in families, in society, at the very heart of institutional power. She is Nana, who shakes up the entire social body with an audacious swing of her hips, giving a glimpse of what must not be seen: her sex. She is Nana, like a Bacchante, rendering bodies feverish while she enfeebles reason.

The Hyper-Eroticized Demonness

The link between woman and nature is not new, even if the nineteenth century lends it modern accents. Already in the Middle Ages it was nature that worried people, as proved by the witch hunts. The witch, through her knowledge of plants and the secrets of femininity, was suspected of having reprehensible relations with nature, indeed, of maintaining an underground cult of nature. Thus she represented the constant threat of the reemergence of paganism at the heart of Christianity; and this took the imaginary form of a return of the diabolical repressed in culture. This threat, which mingles with the womanly being of the witch, focuses naturally on her sex, since it is what distinguishes her from the single being originally created by God: man. The witch's Sabbath becomes, in its representations, an orgiastic ceremony held by hyper-eroticized demonnesses.

A Sex Arousing Disgust

It is generally in periods where reference-points tremble that a fear arises of culture being carried away by the floodtide of an always ill-contained nature, exacerbated by the fear and hatred of the feminine. The late Middle Ages like the late nineteenth century confirm this thesis. The witchs' bonfire meets the Salpetrière hospital for hysterics! The clinic takes over for the Inquisition. It is more humane, but the unavowed motive displays un unmistakable lineage, if only with the practice shared by the high priests of both Science and the Church: that is, exorcism. Let's refer to painting once again. We are all familiar with the primitive paintings where we see an exorcized woman spitting out little green devils, as though the demon rose up from her sex to her mouth, to finally be expulsed. And didn't psychoanalysis, in its beginnings, propose to have the hysteric "spit it out," or in other words, bring the hidden sexual trauma to speech, so as to deliver the patient?

The difference of the sexes (I mean, the difference between man and woman) has always been a subject of preoccupation and no doubt of anxiety; but paradoxically, the suspicion of their relative indifferentiation came to accentuate this anxiety in the nineteenth century. On the basis of prejudice and fantasy, medical treatises long claimed that men and women belonged to two different species. Of course the practice of dissection had revealed an extensive organic similarity, but the idea of an essential physiological difference nonetheless remained a certainty. Man, for example, was warm; woman was cold, which clearly made her closer to the serpent, to whose seduction, need we recall, Eve had succumbed. From the mid-seventeenth century onwards, these chimeras were invalidated. But the more woman was discovered to be physiologically similar, the more it was necessary to distinguish her by making her sex alone into the bearer of difference. Male discourse set to work. It took an interest bordering on obsession in feminine flows, the menses of course, but also the white liquids, the moisture of the mucous membranes, the secretions of the vagina. Classical and Biblical Antiquity knew the impurity of menstrual blood, for which it felt a sacred aversion. This was the register of the symbolic. The nineteenth century found itself possessed, beyond all reason, by an instinctive disgust for this blood that stank, and which, outside the period of menstruation, continued to flow in the colorless form of vaginal secretions. "Woman, sick and twelve times impure," as Alfred de Vigny wrote, became a creature inspiring in man a repugnance that rivaled with his fear of women. All against a background of fascination, as revealed by the journal of Jules Michelet. We enter the register of fantasy. Woman is a pining child who suffers from this hemorrhage that keeps her from challenging man's vitality. But at the same time (the unconscious is familiar with these reversals), the loss of blood makes her an avid ghoul who sucks at men, a vampire in a way—or a vamp, for her bloodthirstiness must be understood metaphorically. The fatality of the femme fatale is thus connected, once again, to her sex. To her sex which procreates and ensures the perpetuation of the species. And as though to add to this register of the disgusting, man had to be born between urine and feces. Thus in his eyes, the female genitals are contaminated by the excremential representation of birth, and by extension, it is woman as a whole who appears to him as a deceitful envelop hiding the wretched substances of which she is made.

Art and literature seek revenge on the male victim of this deception. Baudelaire devotes lyrics to rotting flesh, while others, like Huysmans, describe the purulent wounds of this beautiful body, delivered to its truth by its corrupting malady.[3] The pen and the brush spread pus on the pink flesh of woman, and reveal the canker that is hidden within the indiscreet jewel of her sex.

And so we always return to the female sex, or rather to the sexuality that Freud, against Jung, placed at the heart of the theoretical structure of psychoanalysis. And we return to the Medusa's head that petrified the nineteenth century.

From Jung and his rereading of the myths, another history of the feminine would have emerged. It did not come forth, because Freud was in closer touch with the fantasies of his time. The archetypes would have helped us to hear the voices of the Great Mothers; but they were swept away by the patriarchal, bourgeois vision that left its mark on the discovery of the unconscious at the close of the century. That time is no longer our own. With this critical consciousness of the devaluating oversexualization of women that the nineteenth century has anchored within collective representations, the hour has therefore come to rethink the question of sexuality on a new basis. Transgression, which is only the inverse figure of that to which one remains fantasmatically chained, does not liberate. Nor does provocation. Taking the place of the male voyeur to stage a slit outlined in flesh or to exhibit a procreating belly is not a way for a woman to say "I," to gain access to her speaking self.

On the contrary, it is a way to play the game of the male imaginary. It is well known that the overexposure of the female sex in which certain woman artists or writers have engaged, under the cover of self-reappropriation, merely reiterates the over-eroticization in which man has enclosed women, for her subjection. Conclusion: there is no escape toward autonomy without woman first asserting herself as a subject who is not absorbed in her sexuality; who is not indistinguishable from her

[3] J.K.Huysmans, *Sainte Lydwine* de Schiedam

sex, to which the male imaginary wished to reduce her, and within which it sought to assign her to house arrest. But when we read today's literature, and see the films being produced or the works exhibited, we appear far from such an assertion.

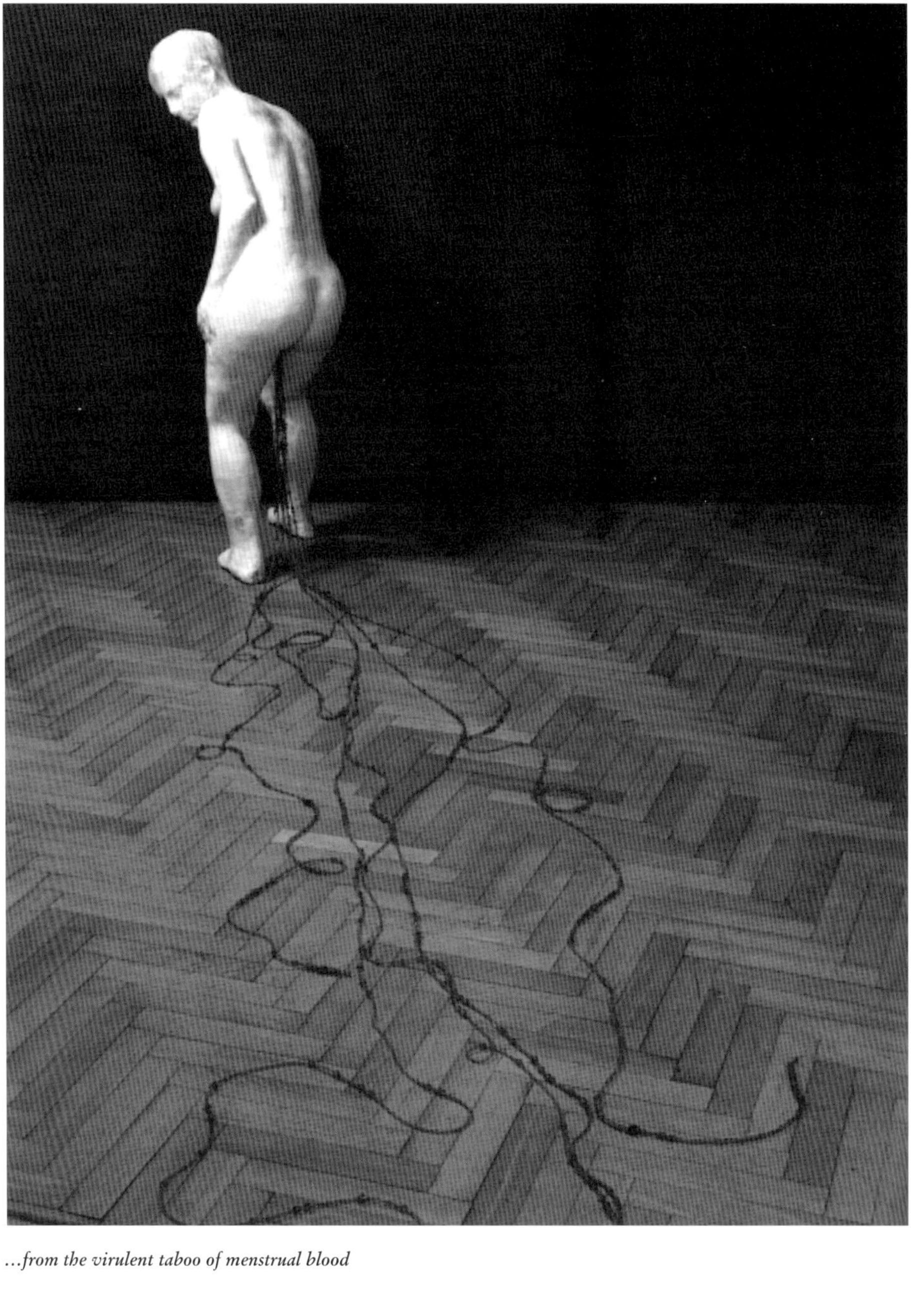

...from the virulent taboo of menstrual blood

World as Will and Representation: The irruption of Women

Only a few were in the know, only a few had been shown the secret of the most famous analyst of the time. For he did not reveal it to just anyone. And why was it this secret and not another, in fact? What led him to choose it? For many years, Jacques Lacan was the secret owner of the famous Gustave Courbet painting that was long believed lost. And it was indeed lost since no one could see it without being shown the master's astute subterfuge at the same time. The painting was in fact displayed in the middle of his living room, invisible, but present, so significantly absent/present. Lacan had hidden it behind a nondescript painting so that he only had to flip it over, to invert it in a single motion, so that what was hidden reappeared, not only for the master of the house, but also for cultural history as a whole: *the Origin of the World,* as Courbet dubbed it, in other words, a woman's genitals.

A sumptuous composition that eludes the representational codes of the period, *the Origin of the World* does not stop at clever suggestions like those of other painters who came before Courbet. Ruebens, for example, placed a subtle arrangement of conch shells with ample open lips in the middle of his series of paintings dedicated to the marriage of Marie of Medicis and Henri IV of France. Courbet's work can be considered literally stupefying in that it succeeds in extracting itself from symbolism and displays a reality on which photography would soon focus its lens. The *riguardante*, the viewer as Nicolas Poussin called her, cannot escape the vision of this vulva roaming freely through the space of the painting. A pink and soft entry into a body that still seems rapt with pleasure in the moment captured for us by the painter's brushstrokes.

What is surprising here is not so much that there was something to hide, but that there was something to see. This sexual organ that nature itself suggests by removing it from sight, this baroque fold, as Gilles Deleuze might say, is suddenly offered up for view, bluntly inscribed in a visual space that is immediately withdrawn. For this painting was curiously as cursed as what it represented and cost Gustave Courbet dearly.

That is why Jacques Lacan's ruse functions as a powerful metaphor. Arrangement of the hidden/exposed polarity has constituted the status of the woman's sexual organs in our Western cultures, as well as the representational order to which they have been subjected, from cave drawings to the present. Nothing of this history can be understood without understanding the intense paradox that forcibly inscribes women's bodies, and especially their genitals, in the dual space of fault and lack: hidden, these sexual organs do not exist. They are a pure ontological absence because they lead to a denial of the very existence of women as subjects. Exposed, they are merely indecency and obscenity, never far from a frantic agitation from which the social body as a whole seeks to protect itself. The *Hystory* of women, I have written elsewhere, is the product of historical conditions inseparably linked to the historical conditions that overdetermine them. Michel Foucault, in his many works, long insisted on the prominent role of medicine and physiology in the various means of controlling the social body. Cultural history wraps its roots around this presence/absence that is both too absent and always too present. If women struggle to defend the rights of their gender, in the civic sense of the word, it is because of this essential tension, this hidden/exposed dialectic that encloses them in the limits of their body.

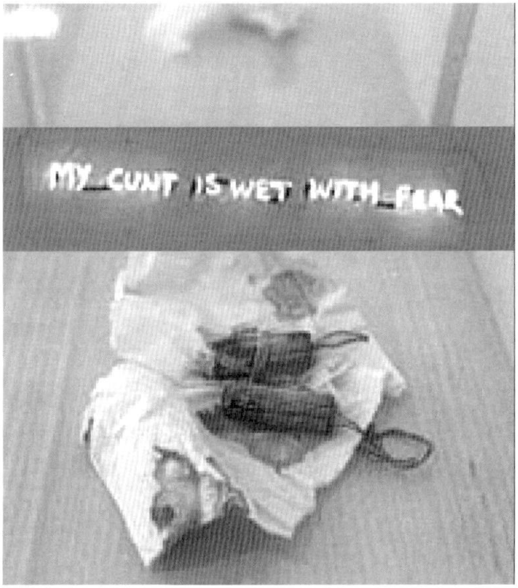
MY_CUNT IS WET WITH_FEAR

The feminine as being-perceived

This question is particularly interesting under the current reign of porno-chic and triumphant advertising. The unveiled, offered, instrumentalized bodies of women are an exact counterpoint to their lasting political and social absence. Overabundant representations of the female body violently reveal its exclusion from the body politic. This exclusion could be concisely stated as: Where there is too much Woman, there is not enough woman. Where the masculine imagination saturates the social arena with its obsessive return to the Woman's body, or the Woman as body, women only have an artificial power frustrated by the multiple obstacles that exist between them and the world.

The best definition of the feminine would thus be: something that only exists to be perceived, *offered to sight*, and this *offered to* signifies the fundamental dispossession of women, the impossibility of their cultural appropriation of themselves. They only exist in this outside the self that fixes them in a being for others. The necessity to be seen, to be in view, in other words to be controlled by male vision, renders the emergence of new modes of representation difficult, even in the vision that women (artists, filmmakers, writers...) have of themselves.

In the movement of this organized monstration, women are the perfect example of the social monster, a creature that only exists to be shown, 'voyeured', trapped in a space where the glance becomes brutal, where vision is reduced to the voyeur. They become ob-scene when thrust into the center-stage of representation in any role other than that of the madonna or the duenna. What could be more indecent than Mona Lisa's smile? Or perhaps the ecstatic saints who from Mary Magdalene to Theresa of Avila sear the canvas with a troubling and violent flame. At the climax of mystical ecstasy, they remain bound, by representation, to the constraints of a gender from which they can in no way free themselves. The great mystics are thus closer to the great hysterical women of La SalpÈtriËre hospital, and even Hildegarde von Bingen elicited conflicting commentaries during her time.

All of this provides an understanding of why art history is full of representations of women in which their bodies—and therefore their sexual organs—play a central role. Reproductive bodies exposing bulging stomachs in Cranach's paintings, proffered chests, languorous poses, or young, bitter Botticcellian girls devoted to purity like a social and cultural hell. Women are without a doubt a good *subject* for a painting, precisely because the technical devices of representation take part in the refusal to consider them as subjects in their own right and arrange everything to display the seductive artifices of their subjection. There are two meanings of the word subject, as Foucault has remarked: the subject of an action and the subjected, the subordinated one. What interests us here, in the case of women, is that the two are combined. But can they really be combined? The history of women is the history of the responses to this question.

Representation of the world and Power

A fundamental question comes up at present: Under what conditions can women today change the cultural modes of representing them? What means, tools or technical devices do they have to try to appropriate on their own what has always been refused them until now?

The world of cultural and artistic creation has in recent years undergone a profound change with an impact on our ways of thinking and acting that has yet to be fully measured. The arrival, if not massive at least significant, of women in realms of activity that had been overtly closed to them. These women writers, directors, artists and performers have started to gain footholds in spheres where the status of creator—although more for men than women—provides important cultural and social privileges. In all evidence, these women have gained a mastery over the different types of languages that they can use to develop a discourse connected with themselves and the world. These languages are symbolic

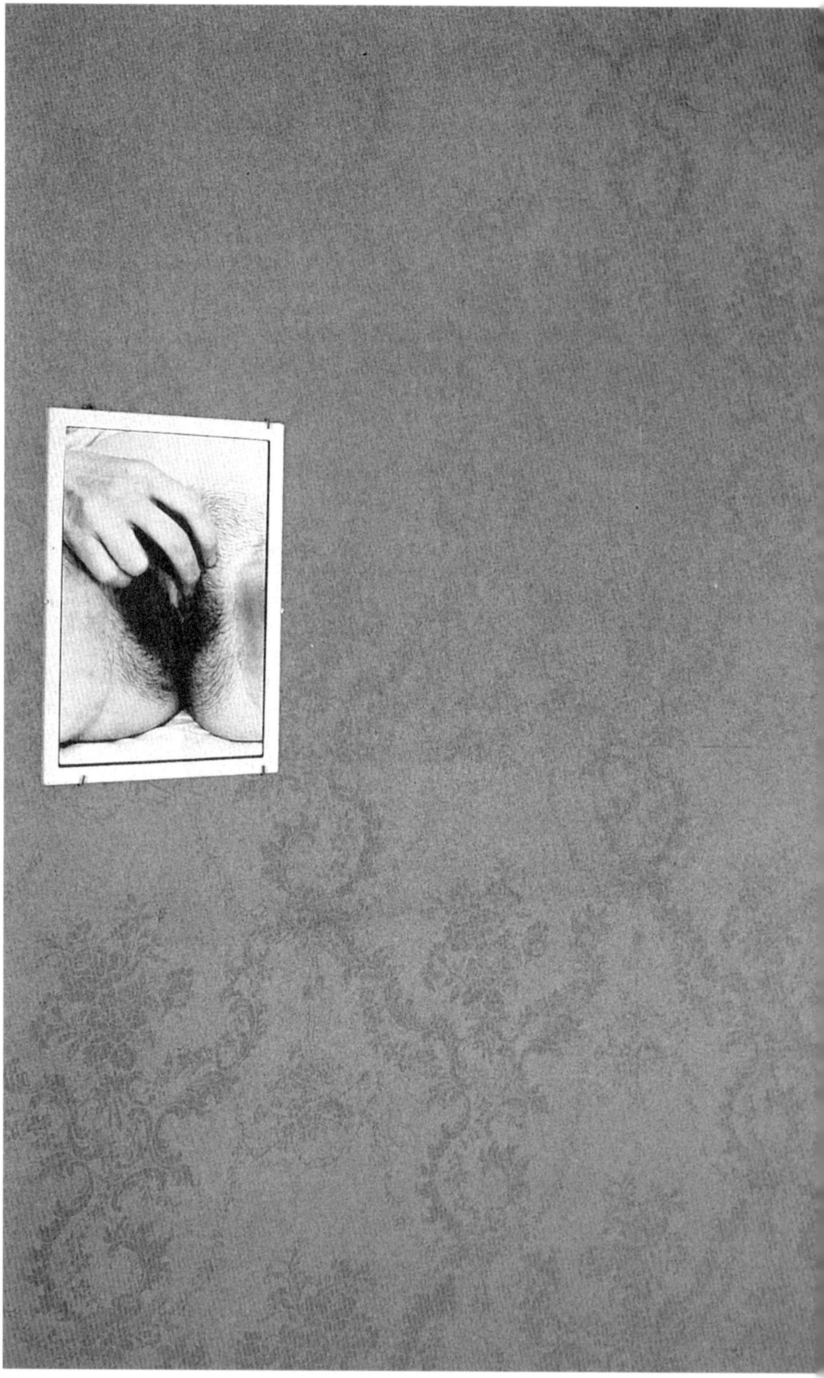

To positively
state one's sexual identity
in the face of
yesterday's vision

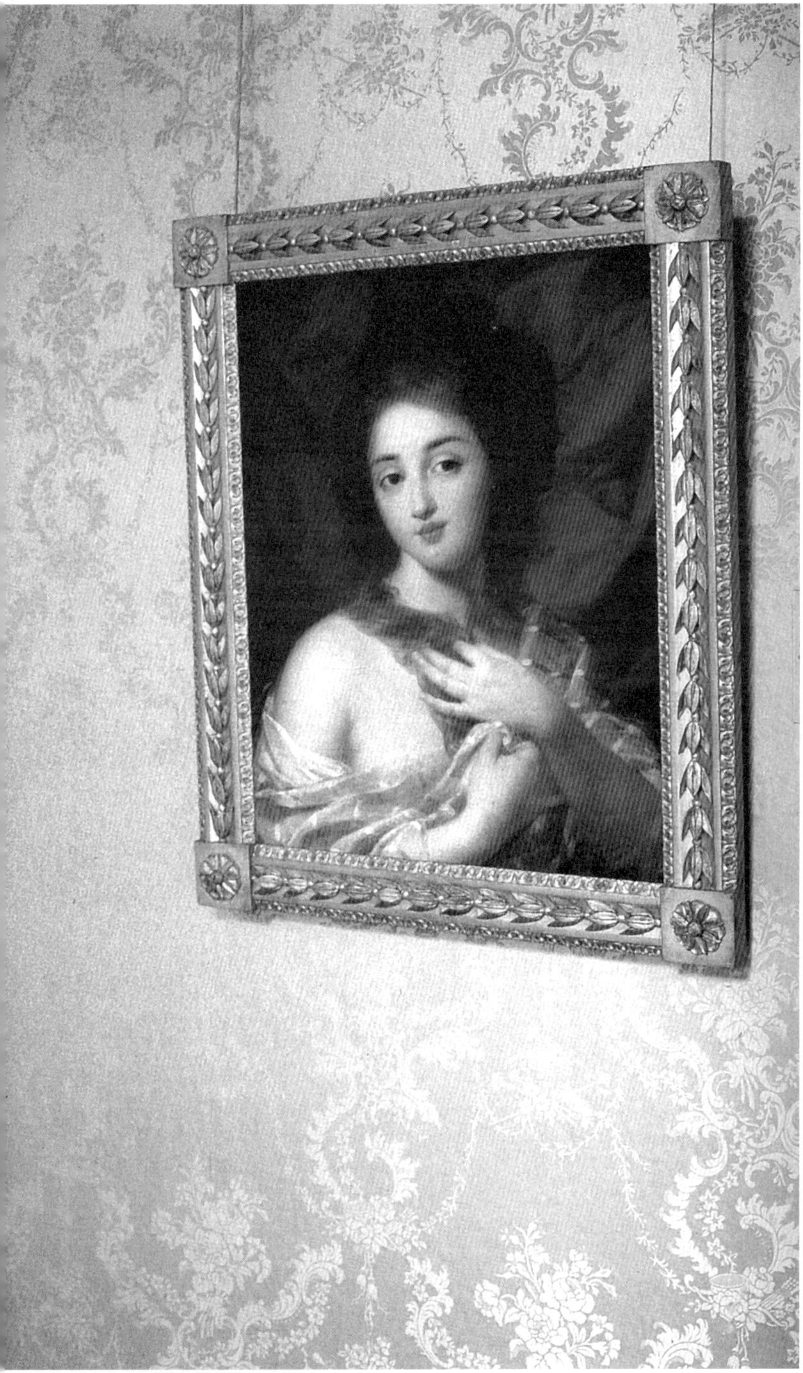

bastions that for the most part continue to be controlled through journalists, publishers, art critics and gallery owners, by men.

Against appearances, the women who create are thus transgressing a cultural taboo that nonetheless retains its strength and efficiency. The sometimes condescending tone of certain media commentaries about the work of one artist or another is still too frequent not to embody the resistance of the social body to what it sees as an unjustifiable intrusion. Virginia Woolf in The Common Reader explains: 'It is likely that in life, like art, values are not the same for a woman who writes as they are for a man. When a woman starts to write a novel, she is constantly aware of wanting to change established values—to make something serious that seems insignificant to a man, and insignificant something that seems important to him. And naturally critics will blame her for it, for critics of the opposite sex will be sincerely stunned, embarrassed when faced with this attempt to change the current scale of values. He will not only see a different view, but a weak or banal or sentimental view because it is different from his own.'

Equal opportunity in terms of artistic creation is all the more improbable than equal opportunity in education, which itself is hardly brilliant. Financial and material investments are more difficult and many gallery owners who do not dare wager on a woman accept to exhibit her work so long as it is put up for sale at a lower price than for a male artist. In the same way, the number of women filmmakers does not at all correspond to the number of students receiving their diplomas each year from film schools. It is true that in the film world, women have the reputation of being excellent editors, a job that requires patience, precision, organization, deference to the director: all the qualities traditionally assigned to women. Film is also more a technical than a creative domain. And that is often where women are put to the test to prove their technical capabilities.

Similarly, in the mid-19th century, one out of three artists was a woman, though no woman was ever accepted at the Ecole de Beaux-Arts or the Institute, while only 7% ever received an official commission or a similar function, even a minor one. For male painters, women painters were merely cultivating an artistic hobby and this idea fed the disdain of the men who entered this profession like a religious calling.

Moreover, the 'youthism' that has stricken the world of contemporary art along with all creative domains and that claims that after forty an artist who is still unknown has no chance of becoming known affects women even more than others. Because the obstacles they must overcome—be they familial, psychological, sociological, economic... —are more numerous than those of their male counterparts, they necessarily arrive later and dispose of an infinitely shorter latency and gestation period than men.

Experimental aesthetics

The dominant trait of these very diverse productions would most probably be found in their experimental nature. Empiricism inherently dominates the gradual appropriation of languages that have remained so protected until now. Whence the prefatory aspects of some works, their incomplete or unfinished character. This also gives rise to the predominant feeling that the women have not gone far enough, that they draw back from a certain creative violence. With a few rare exceptions (Berthe Morisot, Mary Cassat, Judith Leyster), women painters were seldom the most audacious and inventive of their time simply because they did not receive the training to be that way. This idea also helps us understand why literature provided women the chance to rival with men on much more equal ground and to impose themselves as innovators. While artistic creation required a technical apprenticeship and specific know-how, poets and novelists did not require the same training.

The question of the appropriation of these new languages by women is inseparable from the question of the role played by the emergence, especially in the 20th century, of a feminine public. We have little information about women as buyers and consumers of art, even less about the way they look at images and about the kinds of pleasure they take in their observation. It must not be forgotten to what extent this gaze is structured by the dominant norm that renders the idea of a specifically feminine perception of intellectual and artistic productions all the more difficult to accept.

No doubt, when faced with these languages that are new for them, women sometimes lack the culturally customary boldness of some of their male counterparts. But they can also sometimes be found at fault for an excess of violence for the same reasons. Suspected of not transgressing certain taboos as easily as men, they are sometimes tempted to go farther than they would deep down like to go. The publicly assumed violence of Viginie Despentes' book, then the film based on the book, 'Baise-moi' (Fuck Me), probably fits into this pattern. As does the work of several contemporary performance artists who strive to bring down still restrictive cultural codes. The highly stimulating connection between women and Body Art should not be overlooked in this light. Giana Pane or Orlan, to name only a few, have contributed to the legend of this corporal art in which the undressed body, the injured body, the suffering body exulting in its very suffering is none other than the woman's body. Taking one's body as an experimental terrain, creating from this organic material has reconciled contemporary art and women at the expense of a more abstract and sophisticated approach ñ more conceptual, one could even say ñ to artistic practices.

Transgression: a false liberty

Here, the question that is slowly becoming apparent is to know to what extent creative women are still taken in by the ruses of male Reason. In other words, by delving so deeply into the space of transgression, sometimes despite themselves, women continue to confuse transgression and liberty. One is free, one does not become free even by doing

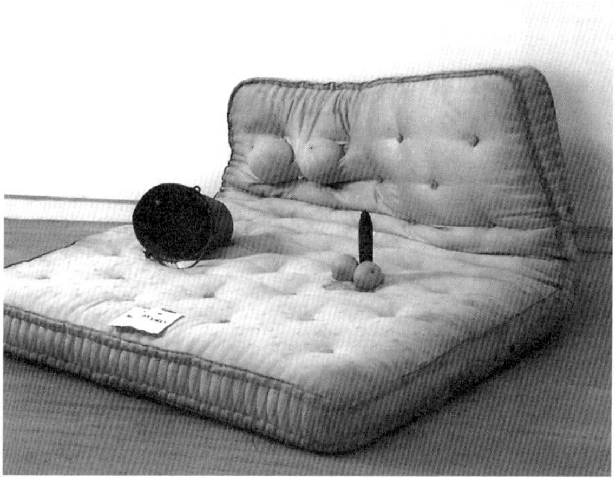

...and facing today's vision
from which
other degradations spring,
like pornography,
which tends to objectify
women's sexual organs...

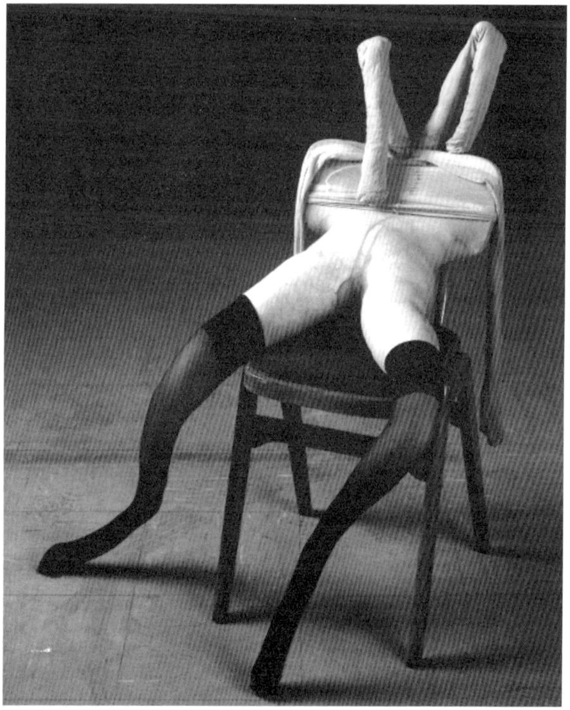

everything possible for it. Like words, freedom is not granted, it is taken, it authorizes itself. Freedom is what a subject proposes who only receives her principle from herself. The knowledgeable and durable organization of women's dependence works to hide this reality: freedom only comes from its own boldness, from the original determination that forms it in principle. Arrogant by necessity, freedom makes no compromises and no concessions. It is asocial in the sense that it founds the social norm and therefore transcends society. If negotiation comes from freedom ñ in using conventions as a means of political action ñ freedom can by no means come from any negotiation. Set down from the start as a fact, it immediately becomes a right. Are women ever for that reason on the side of freedom?

Georges Bataille also described the feminine as a pure power of transgression, a factor of disorder and anarchy. 'The excess that comes with the feminine,' as Blanchot added, is present in all of Bataille's fiction. Each is the story of an eye and echoes the representation of the pineal eye like the unbearable and real image of a blind, syphilitic father. His stories are of an eye that blinds itself in a prodigious vision of bodies, as in the *Story of the Eye, My Mother* or *Madame Edwarda*. Bataille shows us what is fundamental in the subtle link between transgression, otherwise put, woman, the gaze and the body, in other words, the sexual organs. The power of women is here considered and exemplarized as the power to undo, never to bind. Yet Montesquieu reveals to us that freedom, as opposed to transgression, is the power to bind. Refusing this dimension to women means placing them definitively outside the realm of human freedom, and thus from humanity in general.

Woman-world

It is difficult not to evoke in this case the idea of the feminine as making the *world Baroque*. In the 19th century, Michelet considered the

Baroque period as the rise of the 'woman-world'. Overflowing in all directions, breaking out of the narrow confines of conventional representations, elevating destabilization and display as a fine art, the Baroque can in some ways be seen as the height of femininity. By transgressing the classical codes of representation, Baroque works like women exist as excess, an indecent *hubris* shattering conventional forms and the frames built to hold them.

The central figure of the Baroque is really none other than Saint Sebastian riddled with arrows, with his feminine pose and expression of pain on the verge of pleasure. The eroticism of suffering reaches its peak in the ambiguity of this Saint who was for Mishima, as he tells us in 'Confessions of a Mask', the source of his first sensual and sexual arousal. At very the heart of this ambivalence, Saint Sebastian serves to remind us that, throughout Western iconography, the feminine is defined as the bearer of social and symbolic expressions of suffering. Triply feminine by being nude, pierced and in pain, Sebastian is offered to the eye, a martyr to vision as he is to sagittation or more precisely to vision as sagittation. The viewer's position thus combines with the archer's aim in adjusting both eye and arrow. Leading us at the same time very close to the traditional means of representing women. Like a mental penis, the viewer's gaze inspects women's bodies and targets them with the dual aim of desire and perspective.

Becoming a subject of one's story

The question that is then raised, repeatedly, in ever more strident tones, is whether women can escape from the trap that has been set for them from the beginning. What language other than the dominant one can be spoken? What words, what images can be invented that are not an interiorization of male cultural practices?

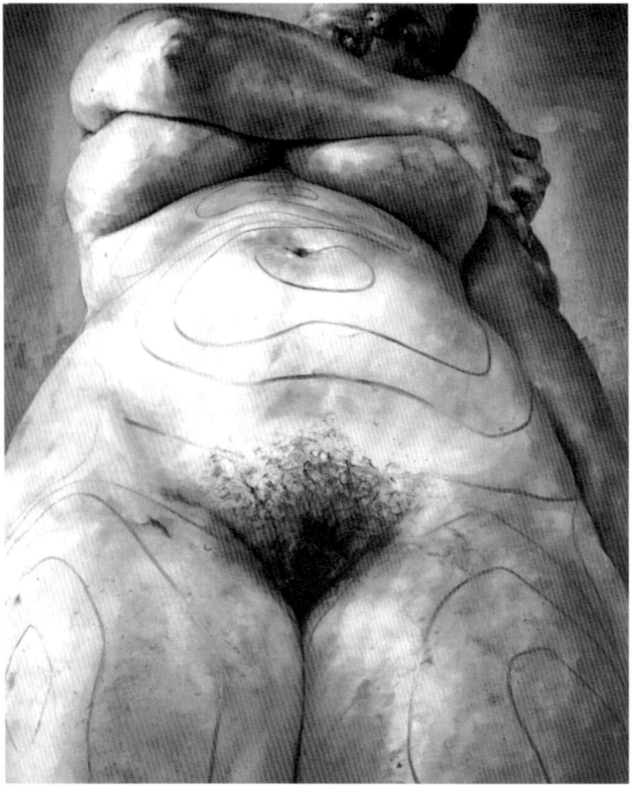

70

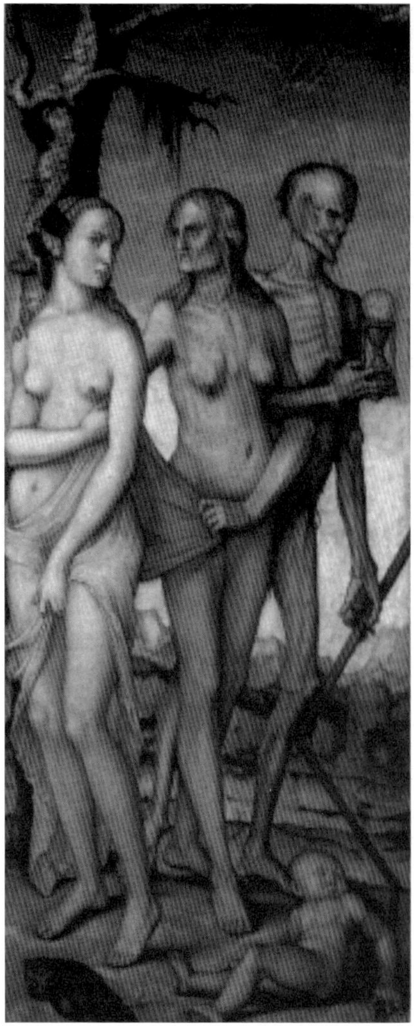

71

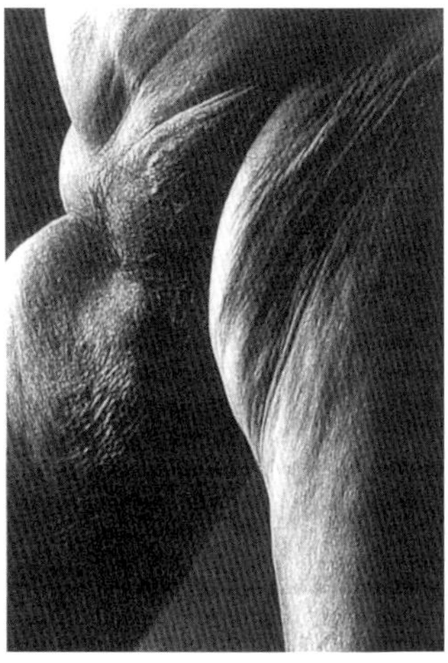

72

...and other offenses,
like a new form
of sexism
of an aesthetic order...

Our knowledge of the past tells us that individuals and communities can only become subjects of their own history by fully assuming *their speech*. Michel de Certeau saw this taking hold of speech as a way of taking power, even modestly, for, as he wrote, 'only power lets one speak on one's own account, to say words oneself.'

How and under what conditions can women produce their own language? How can the invisible (their acting on the world and their status as subject) become visible, and the visible (their bodies and their genitals considered as women themselves) invisible? Women becoming autonomous would mean, as the word implies (auto-nomos), giving themselves, and therefore men as well, their own law. Because naming means providing the law that governs that which is named, women are in the process of choosing the words (and the images) that speak of desire and pleasure as well as of their exact opposite. As if they had to go as far from themselves as possible to find out what they are. But isn't this distant place the closest to them culturally? Stated differently, by exiling themselves in a language that until recently did not belong to them, are women really taking power or are they measuring their impossibility of ever doing so? What lies after the confrontational images, the targeted violence, the inaudible provocations? If the question is to be asked, it must be done with no concessions and in the most disturbing way possible.

That is what the artists coming out of contemporary art are doing today, each in her own way. The work of Florencia Flanagan or Mandy Havers, to only cite a few, display highly interesting traits that are indentical to the ones described above. In *Mother*, created in 1977, Havers created a leather doll with roughly assembled and sewn members. The doll's stomach is embossed with the form of the child it is carrying. Only the head, hands and feet of the child have emerged, intensifying the disturbing aspects of this physical statement. With no legs, thus unable to move, *Mother* remains immobile, though not frozen, on its wooden base, engaging in a strange face-off with its almost newborn child. This unsettling work reveals a confirmed mastery of the materials, while an awareness of the sexual identity of its creator can allow viewers to go deeper and to understand what is implied in the artist's vision of herself as a woman and potential mother. Going beyond mere artistic creation, while including it, the artist creates a sort of auto-ethnography of women.

In the same way, Sophie Calle has for many years spun an auto-biographical oeuvre in which the most intimate details encounter the unknown. Between shadowing and socio-ethnographic inquiry, the artist practices the display of intimate details and voyeurism as one of the fine arts. As both object and subject of her art, she occupies the improbable place produced by the fusion of the viewer, the artist and the work. An inventiveness emerges from this tenacious admixture in which rawness and coarseness serve the urgency of sight entirely. In fact, there lies the true secret of the dominant position. It lies in vision, vision conceived of and experienced as a *Gestell*, an inspection of the world set at a distance and dominated. The voyeur is always the master of what he sees and the exhibitionist is always a slave to his gaze. By claiming that position, the role of the absolute voyeur, Sophie Calle also stakes claim on the place of the master, as both woman and artist. Art as an experiment on the self and the world, this is what women are probably helping to promote the most today. Intellectual and artistic creation has become the laboratory of the self in which women produce veritable arrangements of autonomous activity by giving themselves the right to produce their own representations of the world and of themselves. The implications of sexuality meet up with those of art: it is a question of fighting to reduce the pressures of a social control that keeps women invisible and is still the rule today. Brazenness, obscenity, violence, rawness are all proof that women are no longer playing the game assigned to them, that they are shuffling and rewriting the rules in their favor. These disparate and vibrant approaches revolve around putting the I into play. Singular, autonomous, unique and troubling, each is a lasting access point from which women can reach the status of an independent subject. The demand for a new social organization is emerging from among these

...as the youth cult.

73

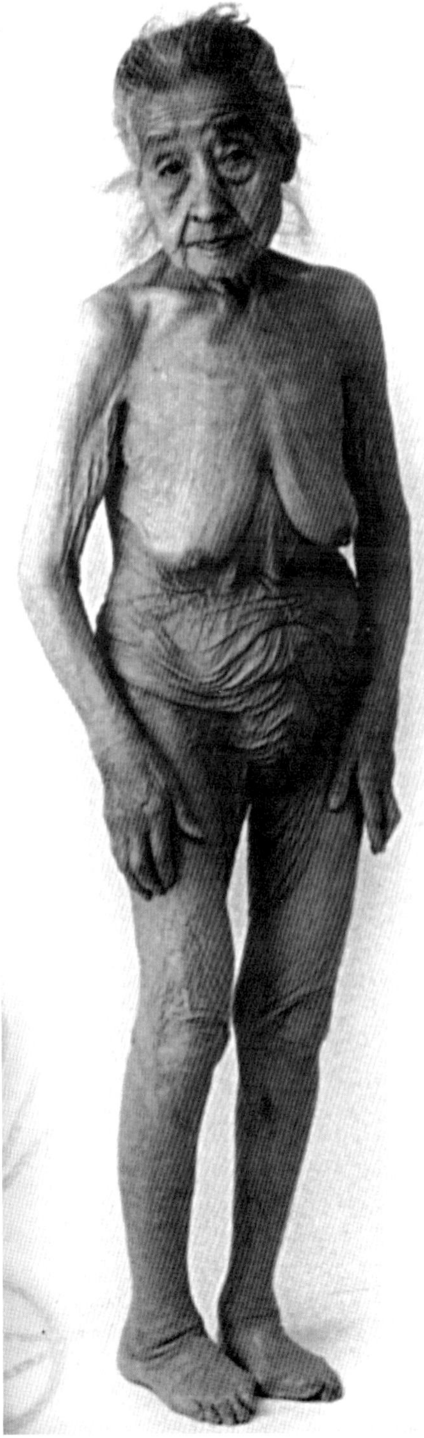

74

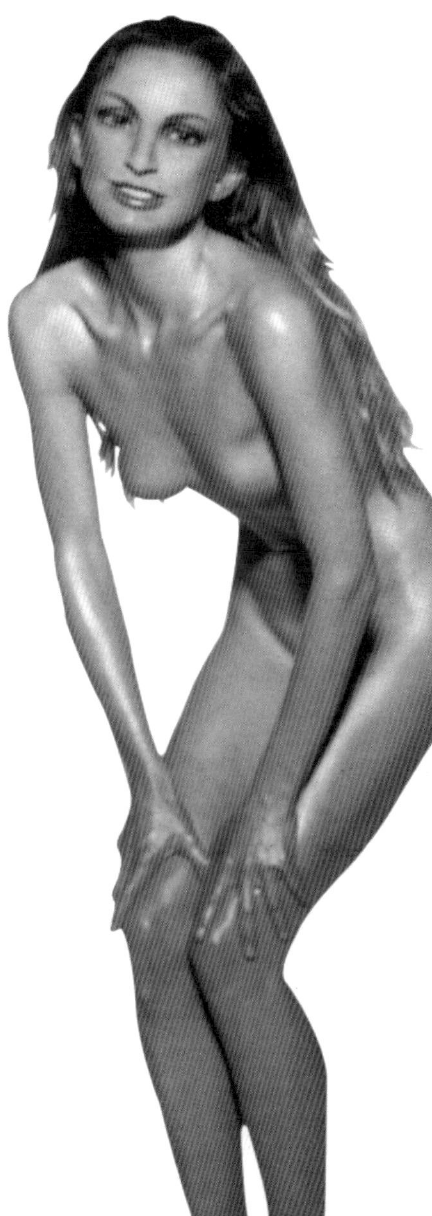

dissonant paths, one that is founded on an aesthetics of experimentation and appropriation.

Art as sculpture of the self.

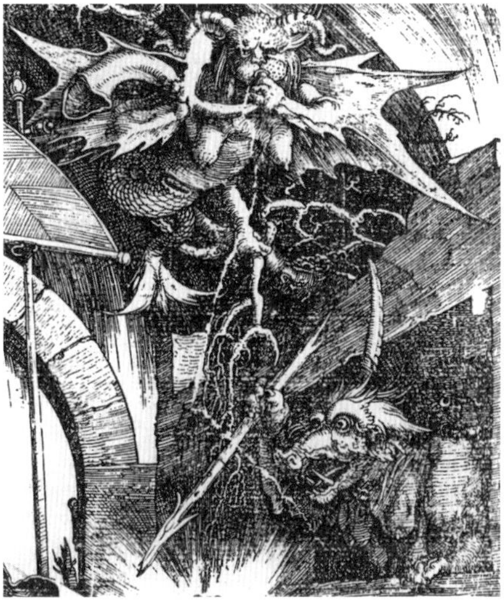

75

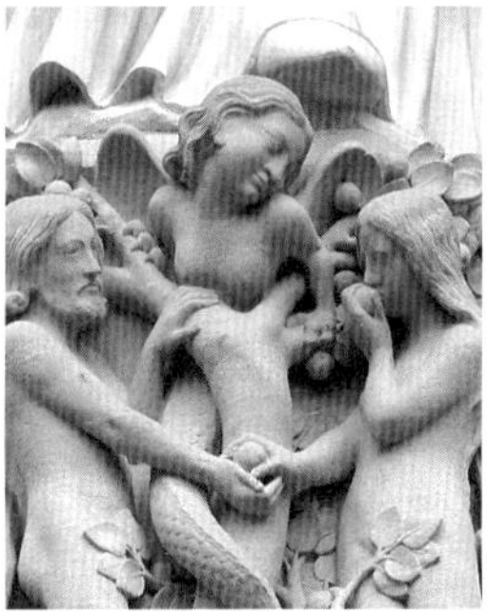

76

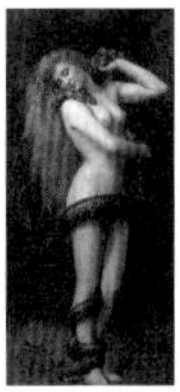

"For what are you blaming me?
I am as divine as Adam.
I was created at the same time.
I am from Fire,
And this Fire was given to me
At incarnation,
At birth,
At the time of human creation.
It is in me as in all creation."
(Lilith)

1) Representation of the Goddess as genetrix of all things, exposing her yoni for the cult (11th Century), stone found in a temple, unspecified dimensions, Alampur Museum, Hyderabad State.

2) Representation of Baubo, the mythic vulva, personification of the female sexual organs.

3) Elke Krystufek, *Share the night*, video, 50 mins, 1997 (fragment).

4) Female form in which the fluidic energies of the Goddess appear. The fifty severed heads that compose her necklace correspond to the fifty letters of the Sanskrit alphabet and symbolize the cosmic powers that preside over creation. The sabre evokes light and lightning. Râjasthân, around 1800, gouache on paper, 30.5 x 20.3 cm, collection A. Mookerjee.

5) Green translucent soapstone statuette, Paleolithic, 6.1 x 2.4 cm, Musée des Antiquités Nationales n°49 281.

6) Figurine of Baubo, Temple of Demeter in Priene (3rd Century BC).

7) Figurine from Lake Trasimeno (on the borders of Umbria and Tuscany), probably dating from the Upper Paleolithic, soft soapstone of a veined greyish-green colour, 3.7 x 1.5 cms, private collection.

8) Chiozza di Scandiano, Paleolithic or Neolithic, statuette in hard brown sandstone, 20.5 x 5 cm, private collection.

9) Gluteal statuettes from Gourdan (found in The Elephant's cave in Gourdan, Haute Garonne), Paleolithic, reindeer's antlers 2.7 x 1.6 cms, Musée des Antiquités Nationales, N°48 617.

10/13. The left hand, despised, reduced to the role of humble auxiliary, designates the sexual bait (more specifically female) of libidinous characters in romanesque art.
Sketches extracted from *la Petite Grammaire de l'obscène* by C. Bougoux, Bellus, Bordeaux 12/1992: (10) Église de Gabarnac, Gironde, pl. XLIII, ill. n°162– (13) Église de Cressac, Charente, pl. XLIII, ill. n°160.

11) Leonardo da Vinci, *Vulva*, 1504/09, pen and brown ink on black chalk, 19.1 x 13.8 cm, Windsor Castle, Royal Library.

12) Léa Lublin, *Le Corps amer (à-mère), l'objet perdu de M.D.*, 1995, model, Mnam-Cci, Centre Georges Pompidou, Paris.

14) Louise Bourgeois, *Le Regard*, 1966, latex and material, 12.7 x 39.3 x 36.8 cm, Robert Miller Gallery, New York.

15) *Christ's wound, breviary belonging to Bonne de Luxembourg, duchess of Normandy*, 1345, illumination, unspecified dimensions, Metropolitan Museum of Art, New York.
Being enclosed in a diamond-shaped form, Christ's wound appears as a vulva. But, by being complementary to the wound, it recalls the gloomy position given to women within Judeo-Christian culture.

16) Workshop of Bernardino di Betto known as Pinturicchio, *The Virgin Conception*, 1490, boards of leather bookbinding, unspecified dimensions, National Museum of Stockholm. The surprising integration of Mary within the God-Father makes a privilege character of the Virgin. It also seems to allude to the intimacy of conception.

17) Hildegarde de Bingen, *Cosmic Egg*, Scivias (Rupertsberg Codex), 1150, in A. Roob, *Le Musée hermétique. Alchimie et Mystique*, op. cit., p.120.

The old cosmogonic symbol of the egg, containing a mixed whole, being the reservoir of all creative virtualities, is definitely reminiscent of the female sexual organs.

18) *The Inferno*, Anglo-Norman Apocalypse, beginning of the 13th Century in Baltrusaitis, *Le Moyen Âge fantastique, antiquités et exotismes dans l'art gothique.*

19) Coptic material dating from the fourth century AD, unspecified dimensions, Guimet Museum, Paris.
The female sexual organs are close to the forbidden fruit, the vulva finding itself simplified in a way as two tree trunks and Eve's crotch.

20) St Pierre de Chauvigny's Church: the toothed mouth of a man-eating monster refers to the toothed vagina, as well as the mouth of Hell.

21) Detail of a miniature extracted from *la Vie et Miracles de Notre-Dame*, XVème siècle, Manuscript Rooms, National Library, Paris.

22) Michelangelo Merisi, known as Caravaggio, *Medusa*, 1596-1598, oil on canvas re-mounted on a wood shield, 60 x 55 cm, Galleria Degli Uffizi, Florence.

23) Pieter Bruegel the Elder, detail from *Lust*, 1558, engraved by Pieter van der Heyden, A. M. Sackler Museum, Harvard University, Cambridge.

24/25 Giotto di Bondone, details from the *Last Judgement*, undated, fresco on the wall at the entrance of the Cappella Scrovequi (Arena Chapel) in Padova (details).

26) Martin Schongauer, detail from *Saint Anthony's Torment by Demons*, made before 1473, mixed technique on paper, Cabinet des Estampes, National Library, Paris.

27) The fairy Melusine in her bath, caught unawares by her master, abandons her serpentine tail to fly in the air (engraving dating from 1517, Library of Decorative Arts)

28) Illumination extracted from the *Apocalypse of Saint Sever* (Landes), made around 1028, unspecified dimensions, Manuscripts Room, National Library, Paris.

29) Francisco de Goya, *Conjuro*, around 1797, Museo Lazaro Galdiano, Madrid, detail.

30) *Lilith / Inanna bearing a lunar crown*, Mesopotamian bas-relief, 2000 BC31) Illustration by Van Maele for an edition of *Satanism and Witchcraft* by Jules Michelet, 1911, unspecified dimensions, Cabinet des Estampes, National Library, Paris.

32) Johann Henrich Fuseli, *Nightmare leaving two sleeping women*, (undated). The incubus which flees on its horse through the window has just "mounted" two damned women

33) Hans Baldung Grien, *The young witch and the dragon* (1515).
The dragon, which is none other than the Devil, attains the sexual act by use of its lingual appendage and thus corrupts the woman; it transmits its satanic powers to her through the branch on which she leans (the Irish word "craeb" which designates the branch, is also used to designate the magic wand). Equally, the smoke which emanates from the dragon's body materializes the satanic lust the woman arouses…

34) Antoine Wiertz, *The young witch*, (1857)

35) Shigeko Kubota, *Vagina Painting*, 1965, Performance at "Perpetual Fluxfest", New York

36) Carolee Scheemann, *Interior Scroll*, 1975, performance, New York

37) Illustration by Jan Ziarnko, extracted from the new edition of Pierre de Lancre's book relating his adventures in the Basque country, Cornell University Library, Ithaca; made after the Trial testimonies (in Candace Savage, Les sorcières, Seuil, Paris, 2000, p. 22, 23.)

38) Engraving relating the story of the werewolves (none other than witches) who terrorized the Bavarian region in 1591, Bayerisches National Museum, Munich (in Candace Savage, *Les sorcières*, Seuil, Paris, 2000, p. 28.)

39) Anonymous, 15th Century, ink on paper, unspecified dimensions, Cabinet des Estampes, National Library, Paris

40) Anonymous, illustration for *Le diable au corps*, 1803, engraving, 21.3 x 13.2 cm, private collection

41) Attributed to François Boucher, *Leda and the Swan,* no date, oil on canvas, 59.5 x 70.5 cm, private collection (detail).

42) Sketches extracted from *la Petite grammaire de l'obscène* by C. Bougoux, op. cit.; Church of Oô, Haute-Garonne, pl. LXXXIV, ill. n°337.

43) Mathias Neithart/Grunewald, *Les Amants trépassés*, 1470, oil on wood, Museum of Fine Arts, Strasbourg (detail).

44) Leonardo da Vinci, *The copulation*, 1492-1494, pen and brown ink, Royal Library, Windsor Castle (detail).

Would a channel exist secretly linking the vagina to the breast? Nevertheless it is the idea proposed by da Vinci to provide against the mystery of the stimulation of the anterior part of the thorax which causes the humidification of the vagina.

45) Katsushika Hokusaï, print from one of the books of *Shunga* (called *kinoe–no–Komatsu*) published around 1814, 25.6 x 17.9 cm, British Museum, London.

46) Giacomo Berengario da Carpi (surgeon-professor in Bologna), uterine system of a woman sitting on a funeral monument, 1523, original engraving hand-coloured in J.L. Binet and P. Descargues, Dessins et traités d'anatomie, p.58.

47) Anonymous, corseted waist, in F. Borel, *Le vêtement incarné. Les métamorphoses du corps*, pl.VI. The corset reorganizes the body image by accentuating the obligatory evasion of the sexual organs, since all the attention concentrates on the waist.

48) *Compressor for ovaries*, Florence Collection (in Candace Savage, *Sorcières*, Seuil, Paris, 2000, p. 71.) The compression of the ovaries is made with the fist or with the help of specific instruments; sometimes the cauterization of the cervix with a branding iron is added, parallel to the clitoridectomy and hysterectomy (extraction of the uterus), practised throughout the 19th century.

49/50) Cathy de Monchaux, *Dangerous Fragility*, 1994, brass, leather, ribbons chalk, two parts of 48 x 40 x 13 cm / 48 x 40 x 18 cm, private collection, London.

51) Scythe in steel and goatskin used for excising young girls in Kenya.

52) Jean-Jacques Lequeu, *Lustful and obscene figure*, around 1790, ink on paper, unspecified dimensions, National Library, Paris.

53) Hannah Wilke, *What Does This Represent? What Do You Represent?* (Reinhardt), 1978-1984, black and white photograph, 152.5 x 101.5 cm. ©2002 Donald Goddard, courtesy Ronald Feldman Fine Arts, New York.

54) Francisco de Goya, engraving, extracted from *The Disasters of War* (1810-1815)

55) Sue Williams, *Try to Be More Accommodating*, 1991, acrylic on canvas, 45.7 x 38.1 cms. Collection Larry Clark, New York.

56) Denise Dax and Eddy Ghilain, *Le grand guignol*, in "Les coupeurs de tête" by Eddy Ghilain, January 1960

57) Pierre Paul Rubens, detail of *Medusa's Head*, around 1618, oil on canvas, Kunsthistorisches Museum, Vienna.

58) Valie Export, *Genital Panic*, 1969, performance, Munich.

59) Helen Chadwick, *Eroticism*, 1990 cibachrome, glass, aluminium, electrical device.

60) Annette Messager, *Sentence*, 1992, embroidered material, variable dimensions, collection of the artist.

61) Faith Wilding, *Flesh Petals*, 1970, graphite on paper, 30" x 24". Courtesy Faith Wilding.

62) Judy Chicago, *The Dinner Party*, (detail), 1979. Courtesy Brooklyn Museum of Art.

63) Martha Rosler, *Bride's Romance Language, or Bianchi Bride*, 1971. Courtesy Galerie Anne de Villepoix, Paris.

64) Martha Rosler, *Isn't it nice... ?* from the series "Body Beautiful", 1966-1972, photomontage. Courtesy Galerie Anne de Villepoix, Paris.

65) Kiki Smith, *Train*, 1993, statue in wax with glass beads, 134 x 365 x 40 cm, collection Mandy et Cliff Einstein, Los Angeles.

66) Tracey Emin, *My cunt is wet with fear*, 1998, tampons, neon and plexiglass. Courtesy White Cube.

67) Zoe Leonard, *Untitled*, detail from the installation at the Documenta IX, Kassel, 1992. Installation in the Galeries de peinture du XIXe of the Collections du Musée de la Ville.

68) Sarah Lucas, *Au naturel*, 1994, mattress, water bucket, melons, oranges, cucumber, 83.8 x 167.6 x 144.8 cm

69) Sarah Lucas, *Bunny Gets Snookered n° 7*, 1997, tights, plywood chair, clamp, kapok stuffing with wire, 101.50 x 90 x 63.5 cm

70) Jenny Saville, *Plan*, 1993, oil on canvas, 274x213.5 cm

71) Hans Baldung, *The Three Ages and Death*, 1511.

72) Yves Trémorin, *De cette femme*, 1985-1986, tinted print with selenium on salted paper, unspecified dimensions, artist's collection.

73) Photo by Manabu Yamanaka, 1997

74) Inez van Lansweerde, *Thank you Thighmaster*, Pam, 1993

75) Albrecht Dürer, detail from *Christ's Descent into Hell*, 1500, engraving, Cabinet des Estampes, National and University Library of Strasbourg.

76) Lilith, Adam, Eve, pediment of Notre-Dame de Paris's cathedral (detail)

VISUAL ARTS

<u>*serie Encounter*</u>

Pierre Huyghe& Douglas Coupland
School Spirit

<u>*serie essay*</u>

Paul Ardenne, Pascal Beausse,
Laurent Goumarre
Contemporary Practices: art as expérience

Michel Gaillot, Jean-Luc Nancy,
Michel Maffesoli
Techno: an artistic and political laboratory of the present

François Dagognet
In Favour of Today's Art

Jean-Yves Bosseur
Sound and the Visual Arts

Thierry de Duve
Clement Greenberg between the lines

<u>*serie monographs*</u>

Marie-Paule MacDonald,
Marc Perelman, Alain Charre
Dan Graham

Gertrud Koch, Luc Lang,
Jean-Philippe Antoine
Gerhard Richter

Christine Savinel, Jacques Roubaud,
Bernard Noël
Roman Opalka

Christine Macel, Marc Perelman,
Jacinto Lageira
Jean-Marc Bustamante

Jeff Wall, Ludger Gerdes, Hervé Vanel,
Ingrid Schaffner
Stephan Balkenhol

LITERATURE/ART/CINEMA

Bruno Dumont
Life of Jesus
Humanity

Raúl Ruiz
Poetics of Cinema

Peter Greenaway
Gold
The Falls
Rosa
Fear of Drowning by Numbers
Papers (paintings, drawings)
Z.O.O
The Belly of an Architect
Drowning by Numbers
The Cook, the Thief, his Wife and her Lover
Le Baby of Mâcon
The Pillow Book
Eight and a half women

Manoel de Oliveira
Angelica

CINEMA

Philippe Tancelin, Sébastien Ors, Valérie Jouve
Bruno Dumont

Jean-Pierre Rehm, Olivier Joyard, Danièle Rivière
Tsai Ming-liang

Jean-Marc Lalanne, Ackbar Abbas, David Martinez, Jimmy Ngai
Wong Kar-wai

Paul Virilio, Carole Desbarats, Jacinto Lageira, Danièle Rivière
Atom Egoyan

Michael Nyman, Daniel Caux, Michel Field, Florence de Mèredieu, Philippe Pilard
Peter Greenaway

Christine Buci-Glucksmann, Fabrice Revault d'Allonnes
Raul Ruiz

Yann Lardeau, Jacques Parsi, Philippe Tancelin
Manoel de Oliveira

CHOREOGRAPHY

Paul Virilio, René Thom, Laurence Louppe, Jean-Noël Laurenti, Valérie Preston-Dunlop
Traces of Dance
(Drawings and Notations of Choreographers)

ARCHITECTURE

Christian de Portzamparc
Genealogy of forms

DESIGN

Pascale Cassagnau, Christophe Pillet
Starck's Kids?
(Beef, Matali Crasset, Jean-Marie Massaud, Patrick Jouin, Brétillot/Valette)

Chloé Braunstein, Gilles de Bure
Roger Tallon

Charles-Arthur Boyer, Federica Zanco
Jasper Morrison

Pierre Staudenmeyer, Nadia Croquet, Laurent Le Bon
Garouste et Bonetti

Philippe Louguet, Dagmar Sedlickà
Borek Sìpek

Raymond Guidot, Olivier Boissière
Ron Arad

François Burkhardt, Cristina Morozzi
Andrea Branzi

Elisabeth Vedrenne, Anne-Marie Fevre
Pierre Paulin

Jacques Bonnaval, Claire Fayolle
François Bauchet

Philippe Pernodet, Bruce Mehly
Luigi Colani

Printed by Policrom, Barcelona, Spain, 2003